Jo Garcia was born in Edinburgh in 1950. After graduating from Oxford she had several jobs in family planning and health service research. She now works on aspects of the maternity service. Her involvement with both the women's movement and with Christian feminism began in the mid-seventies when she helped to found women's studies in Oxford and became a part of the Student Christian Movement. The movement was amongst the first to take up the issue of feminism and Christianity. She is now active in the Christian feminist network, and lives in Oxford. In her spare time she likes growing her

Sara Maitland was born in and brought up in Scotland. She a degree in English Language at academic research, antiques 1974 she has earned her living as a writer and freelance journalist, publishing widely in magazines, newspapers, feminist journals and fiction collections. Involved in the women's movement since 1970, she has worked with groups such as *Women's Report* and Women's Aid. She has been part of the Christian feminist movement since 1978. She and four other women made up the feminist fiction collective whose work was published in *Tales I Tell My Mother*. Her novel, *Daughter of Jerusalem*, won the Somerset Maugham Award in 1979, and her study of feminism and Christianity, *A Map of the New Country*, was published at the beginning of 1983. She lives in London with her husband and two children.

In *Walking on the Water* Jo Garcia and Sara Maitland's intention has been to gather together diverse material that demonstrates the relationship between feminist ideas and experiences and women's spiritual lives – or provides a critique of that relationship. To that end, the twenty-two contributors have produced biography, polemic, fiction and poetry, cartoons and illustrations, all of which grapple with questions of belief in a personal and often provocative way.

Walking on the Water

Women Talk About Spirituality

Edited by

Jo Garcia and Sara Maitland

Virago

Published by VIRAGO PRESS Limited 1983
41 William 1V Street, London WC2N 4DB

British Library Cataloguing in Publication Data
Walking on the water.
  1. Spiritualism
  I. Garcia, Jo   II. Maitland, Sara
  133.9   BF1261.2
  ISBN 0-86068-381-8

Printed in Great Britain by litho
at The Anchor Press, Tiptree, Essex

Contents

Introduction

This is a collection of essays, stories, poems and pictures by women about spirituality. It is about the relationship between our feminist ideas and experiences and our spiritual lives; both in our pasts and in our present. Everyone in the book shares the fact that they take the question seriously, but differs about where she stands. Some would call themselves believers, others would not; but all address this tricky area with courage.

To explain our choice of themes and contributors we need to say something about us, the editors. We have quite a lot in common: between us we have twenty years' experience in the women's movement; we both come from church-going Scottish families and we are both now members (in our own terms) of the Church of England. We have lived lives of considerable security and privilege. (In this most of our contributors resemble us.) We differ too, of course, about lots of things – including some of our political and religious opinions.

We met through our involvement with groups of Christian women who were beginning to present a feminist critique of religious ideas and a feminist challenge to Christian practice. Since the mid-seventies a network of such groups has grown up in this country. Like the wider women's movement, this network is very diverse, incorporating single-issue campaigns, consciousness raising and study groups, ecumenical and denominational groups, newsletters and conferences. This network tends to be ignored by both sides: the churches want little to do with feminism, and the women's movement has wanted little to do with religion. Active within this network, and within the women's movement too, we have encountered women from our own and other traditions who find that this is an important and fascinating subject. Many women, friends and strangers, have expressed relief at finding they were not alone; others have been positively hostile to our paradoxical association with religion. Our aim in putting together this collection has been to expose and develop various strands of the debate about religious faith. This debate is not new, but has recently become more prominent.

This book is by participants (in which we include ourselves) and not by observers. We have tried to avoid theory which is divorced from personal experience. We have used the feminist method of linking the two together. We have included poems and pictures and stories because we felt that this was the only way that some ideas could be expressed and because our contributors chose to express them in these forms.

From the start we looked for our contributors according to a fairly specific plan – although there have been delightful moments of serendipity. Nothing in the book has been published before – many of the contributors have not written anything before. There has been practically no outlet in this country for women to develop their ideas about spirituality. Women elsewhere and particularly in the USA have had a feminist context into which to write about these things, and we wanted to give space to women who have not had it. For this reason too we have not included some of the better known and perhaps more obvious writers – Dr Una Kroll or Monica Furlong, for example, despite the inspiration they have provided.

Some areas of spiritual search have already had attention paid to them by women writing in this country. The politics of discrimination in the Christian churches has been explored by Sue Dowell and Linda Hurcombe in their book *The Dispossessed Daughters of Eve* (SCM, 1981), by Una Kroll in *Flesh of My Flesh* (Darton Longman and Todd, 1977) and in Sara's own book *A Map of the New Country* (Routledge and Kegan Paul, 1983). The issues around the question of women being ordained to the Anglican and Roman Catholic priesthoods have an extensive press; for example *Yes to Women Priests*, edited by Hugh Montifiore (Sheldon Press, 1977). At the other end of the spectrum Sally Belfrage's *Flowers of Emptiness* (The Women's Press, 1982) looks at the phenomenon of 'going orange' and Sukie Colegrave's *The Spirit of the Valley* (Virago, 1978) examines the Tao and oriental spirituality from a women's perspective. Our book is more western than these latter and people may feel that we have paid excessive attention to the experience of Christian and Jewish women, but in fact this reflects the childhood experience of many British women. Women are beginning to use religious forms from other continents and historical times, as well as creating their own; but until we have explored our own historical reality it is hard to move on. We have tried to present some of the new directions in which women are moving but there are of course omissions and discrepancies. For example, many of the women whose experience we wanted to include in the book have not chosen to talk about them in the language of mystery or 'transcendental experience'. Women within the secular women's movement who see the trend towards spirituality as anti-political, escapist and dangerous (a view shared by some of our contributors too) may be relieved to find so little about prayer and meditation, ritual, ceremony, language or magic. While we believe that these are areas which deserve serious exploration, we have followed our contributors' inclination to take up more material concerns and relate them to political perspectives. Nor have we explored the distinction between 'spirituality' and 'religion'. Although we feel 'religion' is the organised, corporate expression of a series of beliefs, whereas 'spirituality' is perhaps something more personal, an experience or sensation that can exist in almost any form and within any activity and without any dogmatic creed whatsoever, the two seem to inform each other even where the individual might wish they did not.

There are, however, even by these standards, some worrying gaps. The community of women interested in this whole area in Britain is predominantly white and middle class, and the book reflects this reality. It is not something we are complacent about and we tried as honestly as possible to widen the base, but we have not been totally successful. For example, despite considerable research – and special thanks to Margaret Watson of Pax Christi in Belfast, who really put herself out for us – we were unable to find any Northern Irish woman who felt able or willing to bring together a feminist and a religious perspective on the troubles in the context of this book. There are also no women whose experience comes from other than the Judaeo-Christian tradition. This limitation probably says more about our insularity than it does about Muslim or Hindu or Shinto women.

However, what we were looking for, and what we offer here, was never meant to be a comprehensive survey of women in world religions. It is the voices of women who have come into the British women's movement for wider reasons than a direct sense of religious oppression, but have found that the issues raised by spirituality will not just go away, all on their own. Spiritual experience, wherever it comes from and however it is expressed, is a part of the real life of many women.

Within the women's movement there has been a kind of shame that this is so, and the shame has led to a denial which cannot be healthy. Over the last twelve or so years we have both learned that silence is seldom useful when the topic is a real issue in women's lives. The issues which concern the women who have contributed to this book are real issues; they must take their place in the acknowledged and confronted experience of the women's movement. Real debate, not a pseudo-tender concern for the mental health of the so-called sufferer, is the best response to women who try to deal with this area of their lives openly.

We are both immensely proud of this book and of all the women who have put themselves publicly on the line about that tricky area – their faith. Many of them have told us how hard it has been to do; and our own experiences confirm this difficulty. However little readers can agree with individual statements (and no-one, including us, can agree with *everything* in this book), we hope that these women will get the thoughtful sisterly response that their courage deserves.

Jo Garcia and Sara Maitland

The Dance of the Woman Warrior

Léonie Caldecott

To be honest, it is easier to approach her from a distance. She is the woman who walks freely, the woman who can be up and gone at a moment's notice. Where I am weighed down with anxiety, haunted by phantoms, muddied by the past, she is as clear as a bell. If you strike her, she rings true. She is compassionate, but not particularly comforting. She is a warrior who has no need of aggression: like the white crane, she brushes weapons aside with her wing. She belongs to the dreams in which I remember how to fly.

In Maxine Hong Kingston's *The Woman Warrior*,[1] she is Fa Mu Lan, who took her father's place in battle: a flesh and blood heroine who cannot be contained in any of the limited roles forever proffered to women. Disguised as a man, she makes love as a woman. She leads her army into battle, yet she inspires and feeds them. The vengeance of her parents is carved in the flesh of her back, whilst she carries her child in her belly.

If Fa Mu Lan is a warrior, she is scarcely a militarist. 'Warfare,' she observes during the arduous shamanistic training she undergoes before becoming engaged in the struggles of the world, 'makes a scramble of the beautiful, slow old fights. I saw one young fighter salute his opponent – and five peasants hit him from behind with scythes and hammers. His opponent did not warn him.'

Which brings me to a distinct paradox in my attachment to the figure of the woman warrior. The fact that I am a believer in non-violence. It is precisely Fa Mu Lan's description of the dishonourable nature of warfare that underscores this for me. The experiences of one of my favourite writers, Simone Weil, during the Spanish Civil War, in which she tried to play her part against the fascists (rather unsuccessfully, it must be admitted!), also have great significance for me. She tells how a young boy from the other side was put to death by her companions because he would not give them any information. She admired his courage, and deeply regretted the treatment he received under the remorseless logic of violence. Later, she was to write the following about the ethics of conflict:

> We should not think that because we are less brutal,
> less violent, less inhuman than those we are confront-
> ing, that we will prevail. Brutality, violence and
> inhumanity have immense prestige . . . The contrary
> virtues, so as to have equivalent prestige, must be
> exercised in a constant and effective manner. Whoever
> is only incapable of being as brutal, violent and
> inhuman as the adversary, yet without exercising the
> opposite virtues, is inferior to this adversary in both
> inner strength and prestige; and they will not hold
> their own against them.[2]

These words sum up my feelings about the necessity for non-violent initiatives in a violent world. How does this fit with Fa Mu Lan marching off at the head of her army in search of the evil brigands? The truth is that it doesn't; but that I can only pronounce for my own situation, and then only in the present tense. Likewise, I can't necessarily take Simone Weil's courageous and difficult life as a model for my own, though I can identify with her spirit (dubbed by some 'the red virgin', she had more than a touch of the woman warrior about her). One of the most interesting things about Simone Weil was her ability to blend the political with the spiritual, a quality I can't help feeling is much needed amongst women if we are to play our role in bringing the world out of the annihilating shadow of a gangrenous patriarchy. Certainly, as I flounder around trying to come to grips with the perplexing issues of our time, the only thing that keeps me remotely sane is that small, still place at the centre, where the committed yet vacillating 'I' who makes mistakes and betrays ideals gives way to the woman warrior.

For me, her dance provides at least part of the answer to the question: 'Where are women going now?' In prophetic moments, I have a vision close to the one described by Monique Wittig in *Les Guerillères*:

> They say, quickly now, fasten your floating hair with
> a bandeau and stamp the ground. Stamp it like a doe,
> beat out the rhythm needed for the dance, homage to
> warlike Minerva, the warrior, bravest of the goddesses.
> Begin the dance. Step forward lightly, move in a circle,
> hold each other by the hand, let everyone observe the
> rhythm of the dance. Spring forward lightly. The ring
> of dancers must revolve so that their glance lights
> everywhere. They say, it is a great error to imagine
> that I, a woman, would speak violence against men.
> But we must, as something quite new, begin the
> round dance stamping the feet in time against the
> ground.[3]

Here is the bright, almost subliminal image I carry with me, an image of my relationship to other women at its best. What we are feeling our way towards is precisely this dance, this lightness, this energy. To be in contact with the rhythm of things, to have a holistic view of life, we have to revolve in a circle rather than marching in straight lines.

The key to the dance is that it is begun as 'something quite new'. This doesn't necessarily mean it has never been done before. What it does mean is that in a difficult situation, a situation where I feel confused and powerless, oppressed by the remorseless linear logic that refuses to make room for what I value, I need a fresh, lateral approach. The woman warrior is a mistress of surprising solutions and unexpected turns. The tougher the problem, the more these are necessary. How to achieve genuine peace (as opposed to the mere absence of war) is perhaps the toughest problem of all. Every time I come to grapple with it, I am confronted by a deadlock of mutually incompatible interests, and I am told, 'Oh, that's human nature,' or 'The balance of power works like this'. WHOSE POWER? I want to cry.

If the powers that be derive their power from gods who have authority over them, then those who resist them may derive inspiration from the goddesses that have slipped from the grasp of authority: the maiden goddesses, Artemis (or Diana) and even Athene (or Minerva). Both are referred to in the passage from *Les Guerillères* – Athene directly and Artemis by implication. Hers is the wildness, the image of the doe stamping the ground, the rhythm of nature, fleeting, elusive, only taken in once the circle is complete and the glance 'lights everywhere'.

To begin my approach to the Gordian knot, I must first face the unknown. I must break out from the sphere in which I have been contained, and for this I come under the influence of Artemis. Nor Hall in *The Moon and the Virgin*, calling Artemis the 'goddess of perilous passage', dwells on the dance that her followers engage in, whose rhythm 'facilitates the passage from one realm to another'.[4] This is the first task of the woman warrior: to make an act of faith, to dance her way into the dark, to lay aside certainties. In short, to become a shaman.

In Carlos Castaneda's books on shamanism, one of the attributes of the female shamans or sorcerers is said to be their lightness. One of them begins her training after stepping, of her own free will, over a line drawn on the ground by another sorcerer. This voluntary commitment to the unknown is the foundation of the woman warrior's potency and her ability to affect things later on. 'Freedom of movement,' says Nor Hall, 'and the undertaking of the great, long walk-about are essential to the wilderness existence of Artemis.' The huntress – or as Castaneda has it, the stalker – is a crucial aspect of the woman warrior. In fact in Castaneda's terms, the notion of being an 'impeccable warrior' has very little to do with warfare, and everything to do with liberation, and in the case of women, their fundamental motivating energy. In *The Second Ring of Power*, the sorceress La Gorda explains that: 'Men have to be hooked. Women don't need that. Women go freely into anything. That's their power and at the same time their drawback. Men have to be led and women have to be contained.'[5]

Perhaps there is a clue here as to the unease with which men, especially men in authority, view the woman warrior. And if she has the nerve to appear in 'real life', she is especially disturbing. A good example is Joan of Arc, who encountered somewhat more opposition than the legendary Fa Mu Lan. Joan is an embodiment of the 'something quite new' that a woman warrior can bring to a situation that appears hopeless, though again she is serving the limited ends of men: the cause of war. Nonetheless, it is interesting to note that she is threatening even to those she helps. The confusion over her role and dress, her insistence on the validity of her own, personal spiritual experience (typical of the woman warrior), arouse deep animosity in those whose authority she flouts. The idea that 'women have to be contained' has turned into the paranoid defensiveness of the patriarchy: should they prove uncontainable, they must be burned. Even the captive amazon proves to be a risky asset, especially while she is alive. Once she has passed safely into legend of course, she can become, as Marina Warner puts it in *Joan of Arc: The Image of Female Heroism*, 'a suitably versatile talisman for a host of causes conducted by men, military and political'.[6]

Another example of the woman warrior tipping the balance in war is the Hindu goddess Durga. The gods are losing in their war against the anti-gods, so they combine their energies and create Durga, who rides into battle mounted on a lion (some versions have it a tiger). Durga is represented in paintings as wielding many weapons. She uses a multiplicity of methods to pursue her goal, and she is never, it seems, caught off balance. Remorselessly she pursues the chief demon, contending with every shape that he assumes until she finally beheads him and thus regains heaven for the gods.

What is there in this story for us? Well, to start with, the fact that the gods could not change their situation themselves, and that they had to create a *goddess*, not another god, to do it for them. In a deadlocked situation, *the woman is the only moving element*. Another thing worth noting is that the dualism gods/anti-gods, good/evil, has a lot to do with the deadlock, a fact which is far from irrelevant to the actual cold wars with which military powers play in the world today. That dualism also makes a point of keeping women in their place, making the female condition the undesirable half of the dualistic equation. The only way Durga can alter the consequences of this division is by employing an adaptability not normally available under the dualistic regime. And here is my paradox once more: although the woman warrior is serving one half of the dualism, she is making a nonsense of the dualism itself in order to do it.

Durga's name means 'Beyond Reach'. This to me is an echo of

the woman warrior's fierce, virginal autonomy. In fact many of the figures associated with her are officially virgin. This is not meant in the limiting sense understood by the patriarchal order, but rather in Esther Harding's sense: she is 'one-in-herself', or as Nor Hall puts it, 'belonging-to-no-man'. More than this, part of the reach she puts herself beyond so adamantly is the reach of society's attempt to describe her to herself. The more repressive the images available to women, the more the virgin condition becomes a defence against these. In extremis, women will reject womanhood itself, if the condition 'unable to move around freely', both physically and psychically, is seen necessarily to accompany it. Although androgyny can become an image of wholeness, there is a stage in which it is primarily a defence, a rejection, even an act of aggression. And in the real world, the woman warrior is frequently a reflection of this embattled state. Before we can find her strong, self-determined manifestation again, it is necessary to see how she relates to the oppression of women, how she responds in captivity as it were, and how she eventually subverts the system that has her seemingly in its thrall, powering herself on its weaknesses and finally breaking free to become herself.

As I said, the woman warrior is frequently found in the service of the patriarchy. It is in this guise that she first entered my own story. Allegiance to the father may entail rejection of the mother, which in my experience was closely connected to rejection of the model proffered to me by my mother in the context of my father's supremacy. Not that the daughter necessarily wishes to be a son instead. She may assume the male guise only insofar as it assures her neutrality and keeps her from being in the same position as her mother. In *The Art of Starvation*, Sheila MacLeod says that she rejected womanhood, 'not because I preferred manhood, but because I preferred girlhood'.[7] If growing up means being expected to conform to a rather limited image, then better to avoid it.

Throughout my childhood I sustained a love-hate relationship with both my parents. They had separated when I was three and, as an only child, I became the focus of their battle to have the last word on my education, my character and indeed my entire destiny. Through them, I experienced the war of the sexes at first hand, all the more because I would be exposed to their respective viewpoints under circumstances imbued with emotional urgency, each in isolation from the other. My allegiance would vacillate from one to the other, depending on whose world-view had captured my credibility at the time. I thought my father more reliable than my mother, because he explained things better, but I clung instinctively to my mother for the chaotic warmth that my father's well-ordered emotions didn't allow for. Finally, in adolescence, I swung entirely over to my father's side, rejecting everything my mother stood for.

During this period, my favourite goddess was Pallas Athene (or Minerva, in her Roman guise). I had always had a fondness for Greek mythology, and in fact largely conceived of life in epic terms, probably thanks to the unpredictable quality of my family relationships. Aeschylus has Athene declare herself 'for the father', a sentiment which at this stage of my life I heartily endorsed. She is the warrior goddess, wise in judgement and canny in war. All these things I longed to be; I was tired of being buffeted by the winds of divided allegiance. I wanted to be on the winning side. She is also her father's favourite, having sprung fully formed from his head, being thus his creation. Feminists have called Athene 'the turn-coat goddess'. Well, I was the turn-coat daughter, incapable of coming to grips with the tangled web of emotion between my mother and myself, and thus taking what looked like a way out. I was going to be the eternal virgin hacking her way coldly through the undergrowth, the clever kid, Daddy's girl.

The solution didn't last long. I soon found myself struggling to avoid being utterly engulfed by my father's world-view. The order and clarity which had seemed so attractive had its highly oppressive side. Once again, I found myself without a home. It seemed to me that I fitted nowhere, and though I have since come to regard this condition as a positive advantage, the insecurity of adolescence was made all the more painful by it.

In her book *The Goddess*, Christine Downing says of Athene that 'she represents just this: the repression of the female and the undoing of that repression as a soul task'.[8] I had to begin the long process of that undoing, and the woman warrior played an important role in making it possible. By remaining with me, growing with me, instead of becoming another reject on the heap of my false starts, Athene watched over my desperate efforts to integrate the divided and warring parts of myself into an organic whole. I have found it more helpful to reclaim her mythology and uncover its hidden meaning, than to consign her to the fire of my new-found feminist indignation.

To begin with, I discovered her mother Metis, the *most knowing of beings*. It is her mother's inheritance that gives Athene her association with wisdom. I realised that the story of Zeus swallowing Metis, or assuming her into his own body, out of fear that she would one day produce a son who would overthrow him, is a clear acknowledgement of matriarchal power, going right back to the story of Gaia – Earth – who helped her children free themselves from the patriarchal prison. Swallowing wisdom is not quite the same thing as generating it yourself, and although Zeus may seem to have assumed Metis' reproductive powers into himself (fulfilling the great male fantasy of creating out of his head – literally), there is a price to pay. Zeus cannot give birth naturally. The image of the great patriarch having his skull cleft open to release the full-grown warrior woman he can no longer contain in his mind strikes me as being not so much triumphant as desperate.

Hephaistos' violent midwifery symbolises, as Noel-Anne Brennan puts it in an article in *Womanspirit*, 'the patriarchal separation of the two hemispheres of the brain, the division of reason from intuition'.[9] This is the fatal dualism which will eventually prove the patriarch's downfall (unfortunately threatening to take the rest of us with him as he hurtles towards destruction).

Zeus feared a son. He did not, it appears, think to fear a daughter. May not this wilful maiden whose cry shakes heaven and earth and who is capable of turning her father's indulgence to her own ends, *if she so chooses*, one day be in an excellent position to lead the old man from his throne quietly and without fuss? She has always been portrayed as taking his side, but personally I refuse to leave her in the hands of the licenced mythologers. Taking up where they left off, I say that Athene is changing sides at last, rediscovering her mother and her mother's inheritance (she has always, after all, been the goddess of wisdom). In fact, by doing this, she is doing away with the notion of sides altogether. If the father must suffer at this time, it is not for some mean notion of revenge on our part, but because he has brought it on himself. Perhaps one day, when the long process of karmic consequence has been worked through, we will once more be able to conceive of what a true and wise father might be. For the moment, the ethos of rabid and decaying authoritarianism he gives off makes this well-nigh impossible.

Once the Gorgon's head is openly worn by Athene, it no longer turns the onlooker to stone. Once I had regained contact with my mother, acknowledged her as part of myself, we both grew stronger and ceased to fear each other. As long as the dark, chaotic, instinctive side of ourselves is divided off from the rest, we are unaware of our own power. It is precisely the dangerous aspect of the woman warrior that will, I am convinced, provide the energy we need to break the dualistic deadlock which threatens to destroy us all. We have to accept and reintegrate into ourselves the dark aspect of our psyche, the crone weaving webs in her cave, before we can challenge the patriarchal nightmare, with its power of terror and despair.

Perhaps we also need to recognise that Athene and Artemis are complementary aspects of the same experience – in captivity and out of it, the one subverting from within the city and the other keeping our tradition alive in the wilderness, waiting for the day when the two can once more be as one (Sally Gearhardt writes about this in her novel *The Wanderground*[10]). If the heavily armoured Athene seems rather unattractive in comparison with the fleet-footed Artemis, it should be remembered that she is also associated with birds. Our solemn goddess needs the flight of the owl and the quick-silver twisting of serpents, just as her dancing sister needs the wisdom to sometimes stay put and come to grips with the problems that require her magical presence. They both need each other. *We* need each other, as women with different experiences of life.

I said earlier that I now perceive my uprootedness as a positive advantage. This is not because I reject my roots (who can honestly say they have done this?), but because in order to survive and undertake the tasks that have fallen to me, I have needed to evolve what seems to be a somewhat fluid identity. The shaman La Gorda calls this becoming 'a formless warrior', and because of it she comes to a point where she can function amongst others with a useful degree of humour and detachment (would that I were more practised in this skill by now!). Because the woman warrior may need to shift her position and set out on a new adventure at any moment, she needs to know the art of shape-changing. The story known as *Meister Eckhart's Daughter*[11] contains just such a woman. She comes to visit the sage, but, when asked to identify herself, replies that she is neither a girl, nor a woman, nor a husband, nor a wife, nor a widow, nor a virgin, nor a master, nor a maid, nor a servant; giving reasons why each role is an inadequate description of her true self. 'Since of all these, I am neither one,' she says, 'I am just a something among somethings, and so I go.' Returning to his pupils, Meister Eckhart observes that he has just listened to the purest person he has ever known.

Purity, like virginity, is a word that has been devalued by the patriarchy. Florinda, another of Castaneda's woman warriors, gives us a taste of its full meaning. Whilst great emphasis is laid on the need for male warriors to rid themselves of the 'encumbering force of personal history', this is not, Florinda tells Castaneda in *The Eagle's Gift*, necessarily so for women:

> 'You see, being a man means you have a solid history behind you. You have family, friends, acquaintances, and every one of them has a definite idea of you. Being a man means that you're accountable. You cannot disappear that easily. In order to erase yourself, you needed a lot of work.
>
> My case is different. I'm a woman and that gives me a splendid advantage. I'm not accountable.'[12]

Women, she goes on to explain, have a kind of invisibility which may be a disadvantage in social and political terms, but is a positive advantage if they wish to disappear and take up a different life. 'Being a woman,' says Florinda, 'I'm not compelled to secrecy. I don't give a fig about it. Secrecy is the price you men have to pay for being important to society.'

The invisibility of women and women's culture is a much discussed theme amongst feminists. Rightly so, since it distorts the way flesh-and-blood women are able to conceive of their lives and potential, and enables men to ignore and devalue the contribution women make. However, purely in terms of the downfall of a top-heavy patriarchal system, I am (as I intimated in the case of Athene) beginning to think that this invisibility may offer, as Florinda puts it, a splendid advantage.

The political implications of this came home to me when I visited Japan and met a young woman who was studying at Hiroshima University. She was acting as my interpreter in a discussion on the role of women in political change, especially with regard to anti-militarism. She told me afterwards that very few of her male contemporaries were willing to engage in this sort of activity, which involves being critical of establishment attitudes and policies, because it would immediately go on their record and jeopardise their career prospects. 'What about you?' I asked, thinking that she was obviously destined for a fairly bright career herself. 'Oh I'm a woman,' she said, 'The odds against me getting a good job are pretty high anyway, so I've got less to lose.'

One of the marks of the woman warrior is that she has little or nothing invested in relationships, structures and values that are extraneous to the task on which she is engaged at any one moment. And in this sense at least, our invisibility is rebounding in the face of those who wish to ignore us.

Ultimately, the woman warrior may have forsaken war altogether. Like the Kalinga women of Northern Luzon in the Philippines, she may one day be able to resolve conflict by going to meet the 'enemy' naked and unarmed. The mere fact that she is herself, unshaped by the game of violence and the struggle for supremacy, going 'freely into anything', as La Gorda puts it – all this symbolised by her very nakedness – will give her a holy power to heal discord. Then maybe she will have to contain herself when it is appropriate. For the moment, we have had enough containment, and the war is not yet over. To be seen utterly naked in present circumstances is a risky enterprise. The eyes that behold us are still those of the pornographer, the perpetuator of sacrilege, full of what Irene Claremont de Castillejo describes as 'inner contempt'[13] for the emerging amazon. These are the eyes of those who imagine they rule the earth.

And yet it is we who, making a small beginning, kicking off our shoes and dancing barefoot on the earth's warm belly, shall draw on her ancient strength to save her and all her true children.

A Sermon Preached at the Women's Mass, Blackfriars, Oxford on 15 January 1982

Text: Old Testament, Micah 4:1–4; Epistle, 1 Corinthians 2:16–3:9; Gospel, Matthew 10:34–39.

Janet Morley

> *What I fed you with was milk, not solid food, for you were not ready for it; and indeed you are still not ready for it since you are still unspiritual. Isn't that obvious from all the jealousy and wrangling that there is among you, from the way you go on behaving like ordinary people? (Corinthians 3:2.)*

On Monday, the octave of prayer for Christian Unity begins. I thought it might be appropriate to anticipate this rather embarrassing week, when Christians are made aware of their ignorance of other people's beliefs and practices, when everyone carefully prays for things which can offend no-one's denominational sensibilities, and then feels relief when it is over. Rare is the town where problems of ongoing Christian cooperation are faced and worked through. In any case, it may be that you feel that denominational splits are not the real issue, and that there is a much bigger divide across the church between conservatives and radicals. An event like this mass would seem to suggest this. In fact, rather than concentrate on how Christian denominations might reunite, I want to look at what we mean by unity within groups, as a starting point for a wider cooperation.

It is a characteristic of all human groups that they want to feel a sense of internal unity and cohesion, and ideally to be at peace with other groups, so long as it is on their own terms. Some of the most moving passages of the Old Testament are those which speak of a vision of peace and harmony, for example the Micah passage we heard read. The elements of this vision are: justice for all, a single ideology, which is Israel's; Israel's God supreme; political supremacy for that now oppressed nation; a peaceful, undisturbed existence, where violence and war are no longer even planned for. There is some doubt as to whether the prophecy is correctly attributed to Micah. The same passage occurs also in Isaiah, and it is quite possible that it was an independent oracle in circulation that was popularly known. It is very much the expression of the ordinary person's longing – for their own vine and fig tree, for peace and quiet. The very anonymity of the oracle testifies to the commonness of the hope. In fact many groups, throughout history, have found that this text and others like it could, just as they stand, express their own hope. A recent example would be the Rastafarians, for whom Africa is the new Zion. For the Jews, this longing, common to all groups, especially those struggling for identity and survival against external threat, crystallised in a definite Messianic belief.

For the Christian church, too, in its early days, unity and cohesion were a strong concern, but the issues were subtly different. Still we have a persecuted, struggling minority, but the ideology has significantly changed, as far as the nature of the group is concerned. There is still an eschatological expectation, but the church does also have the responsibility to 'be' the Messianic community, to demonstrate that Christ has made a difference. Paul, in the passage we heard from Corinthians, is encountering the problem that remains ever with us: that the church ought to be spirit-filled, and in fact, to his and our frustration, persists in behaving like an ordinary human institution with ordinary people in it. There are splits, wrangles, divisions and power-struggles.

A common reading for Christian Unity week that I refrained from choosing is the prayer of Christ for unity, John 17 v 21:

> May they all be one.
> Father, may they be one in us,
> As you are in me and I am in you,
> So that the world may believe it was you who sent me.

This passage is very guilt-inducing, and I think guilt can be a positive barrier to unity. The problem is that Christian groups, concerned with being that which would mark them out as distinctively Christian, try to 'be' what they ought to be without going through the painful process of becoming that. The church, like any other human institution, has tended to assume unanimity, and when internal conflicts have built up to a point beyond ignoring, has split, with either side of the split, of course, believing that they are the One True Church.

I want to look at some of the ways in which the churches, both denominations and more informal groups, have tried to assume an internal unity in an unexamined way, and here I have found theories of group process to be illuminating.

One way is that the group acts as if it were totally dependent on a strong leader.

This behaviour is obvious where hierarchical leadership is part of the official theology, for example within the Catholic Church. But it can also been seen in cases of dramatic charismatic leadership such as John Wesley's. When this type of leadership is good, the results can be dazzling; the group is attractive to many people, and many projects get off the ground. The group, because it looks upwards for initiatives and decisions, is aware of no dissident voices. Part of the reason you join such a group is the sense of oneness of purpose. Those who can't accept the authority of the one at the top either don't join or else generally leave. In the members of the group, dependence is displayed. It is relatively easy to point this out, and indeed to criticise it, in overt hierarchical structures. However, dependence also occurs where hierarchy has theoretically been rejected by the group. Non-conformists, part of whose creed was to throw out the authority of a priestly caste, will still often react to their minister in the same way as a Catholic parish to its priest: 'The church ought to be making a stand' – their minister ought to have written a letter to the paper. It is much harder to discuss the issue of dependence when the group officially doesn't behave that way.

What is wrong with dependence as a means to unity? For one thing, if the leader departs, the group must have a replacement who works in a similar way, otherwise the group collapses. Factions emerge, which couldn't surface before, or paralysis sets in – no-one knows how to make decisions collectively.

Talking of collective decisions, it is worth considering how women's groups operate, whether Christian or not. It is part of feminist philosophy that we don't work hierarchically; hierarchy is identified with masculine culture. So what happens? In my experience, it is possible for groups to be half-paralysed from the start by the ideology that women inherently have new and non-dominating ways of relating to each other in groups. Leadership becomes an embarrassing topic to discuss in depth; meanwhile, one strong personality, or maybe a few articulate women, will tacitly be granted power. She or they will tend to convene meetings, define the issues, and talk most frequently (often stressing that no-one, of course, is trying to dominate the group). She will be moaned about by individual members, but seldom challenged in the group. The problem can become unnameable, because there isn't supposed to be a problem – we left it outside the group with the men. The result is that the group often talks about making decisions or taking action, but finds it very hard to do so. It can neither take a collective decision nor admit openly that it wants its more influential members to act on its behalf.

Another basic assumption that a group often makes in its search for unity is fight/flight behaviour. In this phase, a group feels itself to be united because it has identified a common enemy, external to the group. The church as a whole has frequently gone for this option. At first, this was realistic. Martyrdom was no fantasy, but a real possibility. But it still remains as a solid part of Christian mythology, even when Christianity has been the state religion with actual political power, that the church is embattled against the world. In our hymns, the theme of battle, of fighting an enemy, is very popular. This image has been taken up much more frequently than the pastoral or organic images for community found in the New Testament. The Church as Army is a common metaphor.

Groups which are set up in opposition to a dominant group, radical groups, are particularly prone to getting stuck with the type of unity that is achieved by a battle mentality. Here I must stress that I am not underestimating the actual evils which such groups set out to oppose. Sexism and racism, for example, do exist and need fighting. But there is a danger in relying on the existence of the enemy for the group's survival and unity. First, the enemy tends to assume demonic proportions in the group's thinking, thus justifying any kind of attack. Second, it is fatally easy for us to project on to the enemy those qualities which we cannot accept in ourselves (e.g. domination for feminists). The point of Sydney Carter's hymn, 'The Devil Wore a Crucifix', is this: not that factions and parties are all devil-inspired, and that no-one should organise or unite at all – rather that naming the enemy as, by definition, outside our group, is destructive and deluded.

Being a member of a group that is fighting for a cause is exhilarating – the sense of solidarity, of marching shoulder to shoulder with comrades, is inspiring. But it is important also to see how the group reacts to an internal threat to its unity. An embattled nation is likely to sniff out treachery, and an embattled church is going to be preoccupied with heresy, and start witch-hunts. A group whose main culture is to fight an enemy is severely threatened by dissidence within its ranks, especially if what is being questioned is the group's ideology about the enemy – that is, if someone in the group attempts to put the enemy's point of view. A common reaction of this sort of group is, rather than allowing its beliefs to be modified, to set about redefining the boundaries of the group so as to exclude the dissident members and thus preserve its 'unity'. A particularly extreme example of this is Mary Daly's community of Hags, as defined in her book *Gyn/Ecology*.[1] Here, not only are men seen as totally and irredeemably evil, but most women and indeed most feminists, are only 'token' women, so corrupted are they by the enemy.

In a less dramatic form, many of you will have experienced the 'more radical than thou' or the 'more feminist than thou' syndromes. Alongside the warm solidarity goes an anxiety in each group member – 'Will my latent conservatism be suspected?' 'Will the group accept me as sufficiently feminist?' I can't be the only person who has clasped her hands to conceal her wedding ring when sitting in a particularly radical feminist group. And of course there are groups at the other end of the Christian spectrum which make anxiety-producing distinctions between 'real' and 'token' Christians. Group members will tend to produce evidence in discussion of their ideological purity, and hence their right to belong to the group.

Speaking of which, I think it is no coincidence that the great creeds of the church were formulated at times when heresies threatened. And concern with doctrine leads me to a third point about the unconscious ways in which a group pursues unity.

The assumption is that unity is achieved by avoiding differentiation within the group, that the whole point is to behave as if the group were one big undifferentiated mass, all thinking and believing exactly the same things. All one big happy family. In fact, the family as we know it is a good example of this kind of culture, and it is no surprise to find that the church is very fond of using family metaphors to refer to its own dynamics. Families, though not normally holding official creeds, often have very strong unwritten ones that correspond closely to our society's myths about warm, close family life, free from conflict. Families frequently take it for granted that the interests of each member are the same as those of the group, and that many assumptions will unquestionably be shared. These may include political and religious beliefs, but more subtly, and more powerfully, it will be agreements about how the family operates – 'Thank goodness we don't have rows in this family' (not like next door). This sort of observation amounts to a creed you'd better not ignore. Since the adolescent's task is precisely that of differentiation, this is painful to all concerned, and sometimes seen as breaking up the family.

Many children, when they are grown up, find that the only way of preserving the family atmosphere on visits home is to avoid certain topics. Hence Christmas can be a strain; since it is a time when everyone is making a special effort to be what the family ideology dictates – united – but as a group it feels too painful to risk looking at our differences in a way that might actually achieve that. It is the same with the Christian family; we have a frustrating sense of trying to live out our ideal as a group before we have the necessary maturity.

To go back to the vision we began with. The crucial thing about Micah, as about the other prophets, is that the promise of ultimate harmony is never offered without the fiercest self- criticism. If we reflect on the political situation in which the prophets gave their message, this becomes all the more astonishing. The nation was embattled; there was a threat from Assyria that made Israel's very survival precarious. This was the moment that the great prophets chose not to issue rallying cries of the 'unite against the enemy' variety, but ruthlessly to castigate the country's internal oppression, to expose the vast difference in interest between the rich and the powerless, and to criticise prophets who cried, 'Peace, peace,' where there was no peace.

As we have seen, to be such a voice at such a time is dangerous – one is open to accusations of treachery. The prophet Jeremiah did suffer imprisonment on this account. Prophets were seen as destructive, an internal threat to unity, subversive. But in my mind it was undoubtedly the capacity of the Jewish nation eventually to internalise and revere this self-critical tradition that made it able in fact to survive as a group through defeat, destruction of its political and religious capital, and exile.

As Rosemary Ruether has pointed out,[2] it has been the habit of the church from earliest times to appropriate to itself the prophets' vision of a fulfilled Messianic community, and to apportion to the Jews the prophetic criticism of Israel's human failings. This resulted in some scandalous historical justifications for oppressing Jews, and also deprived the church of the prophetic heritage of internal criticism. This is a heritage we need to reclaim; a vague sort of pious hopefulness is not going to make the church a symbol of the Kingdom of God, if we allow our institutions to function, unchallenged, just like any human groups do.

The world more urgently than ever needs a workable model for achieving harmonious relations. 'Taking a stand on world issues' on the part of the church fails to convince if we leave our own power structures unexamined. This is one reason why it is crucial for radical Christian groups to stay firmly within the church. But the model operates one step down also. A radical group that works from a self-righteous standpoint, settling for one or other of the precarious, and finally spurious, types of internal unity I have described, does not offer a prophetic criticism to the church. It simply reflects the culture it is attempting to reform.

I want to turn finally to the gospel passage. Jesus is here quoting from Micah, and it is a passage that is much more typical of the prophet than the one we heard read: 'I have come to set "a man against his father, a daughter against her mother, a daughter-in-law against her mother-in-law. A man's enemies will be those of his own household." '

In Micah, the context is his diagnosis of the corruption within his society and the words are found alongside accusations of perverted justice and abuse of authority. Jesus is apparently altering the meaning to refer to the divisiveness of his own presence, and this interpretation was current at his time within the Messianic predictions. It was said that Messiah's coming would produce a situation of crisis, revealing divisions in relationships thought secure. In any case, Jesus stands solidly within the prophetic tradition of requiring those who want an easy peace to face the reality of division and conflict.

It is interesting that, in Matthew, the saying is found next to the one about losing one's life in order to save it. I want to suggest that this painful necessity applies as much to groups as to individuals. It can feel like death in a group to give up our easy solidarity and our survival techniques, in order to focus on our undercurrents of conflict, but it is the only place to start the search for a lasting unity.

Growing Up Jewish

'Elizabeth'

I grew up in London in the sixties. I was not part of the generation of Jews who struggled against poverty and extreme anti-Semitism or who had lived through the Holocaust in Europe. I was part of the next generation. We were the ones who had been struggled *for*, the ones who should have been grateful – grateful for survival and grateful for the material standards our parents had achieved. How could such a struggle ever be repaid? Could a Jewish child ever feel worthy of so much suffering?

I received the same message as most non-Jewish girls – 'be a good daughter, a good wife, a good mother'. It just seemed to come with a higher intensity. Much as I would like to, I cannot escape even now the feeling that a woman without children is incomplete. A boy learns to serve God through religious observance and study but a girl is taught to serve God through duty to her family. From early on she absorbs the concepts of duty and guilt – the guilt of failure in her duty. There is an element of paradox in the low status of women in Judaism. A woman confers Jewishness on her children while a man does not. There are plenty of jokes and anecdotes about the powerful Jewish mama who is totally in charge of her home. But, overall, the image of Jewish womanhood is a glorification of servility.

As in all good patriarchal cultures, a daughter is a pretty second-rate thing. My parents produced two of them, and after a while it became clear that that was all they were going to get. We were given very confused and confusing messages by our parents. As well as being dutiful daughters we were to fulfil their ambitions as surrogate sons. We were expected to be inquisitive, ambitious, independent; to use our education to the full and then excel in our chosen careers (without having the freedom to explore the possibilities). At the same time we had to be modest, model, unquestioning young women just waiting for the first Mr (Jewish) Right to come along and fall dreamy-eyed into his deep-freeze and eye-level oven. With his highly paid professional job we would never have to 'work' again. Consequently, in our parents' eyes, educational achievements were both expected, and dismissed as being too clever. Our chosen careers were irrelevant but not ambitious enough. No man was ever good enough but we really ought to have one!

The other messages from my childhood are of being Jewish in a frightening, hostile and basically different outside world. Emotionally, a Jewish child still felt in a ghetto. I cannot remember a time when I was not conscious of being Jewish. I remember feeling very different in junior school. Someone there once told me that I, personally, had killed Jesus and I was quite upset at the accusation. It felt awkward to visit the homes of non-Jews. I remember thinking that non-Jewish homes even smelled different. Worry about the dietary laws was part of the problem. One Passover I stayed at a schoolfriend's home and ate a biscuit by mistake. A biscuit counts as leavened bread and for ages I felt that something terrible might happen to me.

I suppose that for the first ten years or so it is the family that make the choices that set a Jewish child apart – she absorbs, but has few areas of control. The family may live in a Jewish neighbourhood and have mainly Jewish friends. They may go to synagogue every Shabbat (Sabbath) or only for the main festivals.

They may keep kosher with varying degress of strictness from simply avoiding pork and shellfish to having separate crockery for milk and meat dishes. They may send their children to Cheder (Jewish Sunday school) at the synagogue and a few may send them to Jewish day- or boarding-schools.

My parents both came from large and very orthodox families, where all festivals and religious practices were strictly observed. They are untypical in that they come from very different Jewish communities with distinct customs and traditions, though sharing the same basic religious beliefs. My mother's family were Sephardi, the culture of Middle Eastern Jews and of old established Spanish and Portuguese families. Her parents were from Iraq. They settled and brought up their children in India and she came to England in her twenties. The language of the older people in the community is a form of Arabic, and she spoke both English and Arabic at home. My father, on the other hand, was brought up in the East End of London, and his family, like the majority of British Jews, come from the Ashkenazi tradition of Eastern Europe with Yiddish as their common language.

My parents chose for themselves a more relaxed and convenient version of Judaism, which combined a few customs from both communities, together with the main practices common to both. They keep kosher to a degree, buying only kosher meat and not mixing milk and meat products in one meal, but not to the extent of having separate sets of crockery. They observe the main festivals, and light candles on Erev Shabbat (Friday night). They often expressed the idea that the religious practices were really 'for the children' – which meant, I suppose, that they wanted to ensure that we appreciated our Jewishness and had some knowledge of our history. As we grew older, the minor festivals such as Chanukah and Purim were rarely even mentioned and they seemed to derive little real pleasure from the main ones such as Rosh Hashana (the New Year) and Pesach (Passover). I remember going through a very pious phase at about nine or ten, largely due to the indoctrinatory nature of Cheder. I felt torn between the embarrassment of informing my parents that I had to keep the Sabbath and go to synagogue and so on, and the sin of going shopping for my mother on a Saturday – and, worse still, 'being seen' at the shops.

Most Jewish families live in the main cities and tend to be concentrated in particular areas. The experience of growing up in a Jewish family which is fully integrated into the community, or alternatively in a very orthodox family, would be quite different from mine. I feel that I can only write about personal impressions and accept that my interpretation of Jewish ideology is based on very sketchy knowledge. However, I think it is fairly typical of the grasp of Jewish knowledge and experience that the majority of Jewish children gain in a few years of Cheder and irregular attendance at synagogue. It is from such simplistic conceptions and misconceptions of religious beliefs and practices that most of us evolve a religious identity.

I found that I became more conscious of the religious part of being Jewish as I grew older. As a child, a lot of Jewish law felt like an inconvenient restriction with no comprehensible purpose – like not being able to 'work' on Shabbat and festivals. 'Work' means spending money, travelling by car or bus, writing, watching TV, as well as actual work. So growing up involved a rejection of the practices without ever having seen any relevance in them. I certainly cannot believe that there is anything intrinsically holy in keeping up a lot of complex practices in order to please some externalised spiritual being. But I have gradually found that in all the practices there is an element which is nourishing to something inside me though I'm still not self-disciplined enough to observe them all. As a child, Yom Kippur, the annual fast and Day of Atonement, and the most important festival of the year, was an occasion for walking around the neighbourhood, from one synagogue to another, to chat to friends and to fantasise about food, counting off the hours until we could legitimately eat and drink again. As I grew up I actually began to look forward to Yom Kippur rather than dreading the discomfort of it. It seemed quite wonderful to have one day set aside to think about the past year and to plan for the next. I found it quite a relief to have that space without the familiar props and distractions of working and eating. It felt like a socially accepted custom for extreme self-indulgence. I also remember that I found my grandfather's practice of reciting the *bruchas* (blessings) quite bizarre. There are specific blessings for almost every daily act, getting up, eating and drinking particular foods, washing, going out, coming in, going to sleep. I now wonder whether this practice could become an immense celebration of existence, a continual reminder of the now-ness of everything we do. If we were conscious of each occasion that we had water to wash with or food to eat, could we still participate uncritically in systems that allow a large proportion of people to have neither?

We lived in an inner London suburb with a fair-sized Jewish community in the surrounding area. I went to the local junior school where there were only a handful of Jewish children, but not so few that I felt odd. I had both Jewish and non-Jewish friends. It wasn't until secondary school that I was aware of making choices about friends or social life. In a comparatively large school it seemed easiest to gravitate towards the other Jewish girls as immediate and safe contacts. It turned out that they provided the most constant and deep-rooted friendships. The school was quite far from home and was for girls only and so at around twelve or thirteen it seemed important to find another base for my social life. It was inevitable that this should be a Jewish one. There was also the expectation that I should only go out with Jewish boys. There seemed to be two main options for the Jewish teenager – the synagogue and the youth movements. I tried out both for a while but then found I had to settle down in one or the other. It was difficult to become well integrated in both.

Traditionally the synagogue has been the focus of the Jewish community, a centre for social organising, study and welfare work as well as prayer. In the past it was the preserve of men. I used to think that this was because of the Jewish notion of a woman's 'uncleanness' during menstruation. Natalie Rein offers another explanation in her book *Daughters of Rachel*, invoking woman's separate role in society. She quotes Rabbi Dr Isadore Epstein:

> This exemption is not a mark of women's inferiority but is in accordance with the Talmudic principle that one who is engaged in one religious act is exempt from claims of another on him. The vocation of womanhood is itself considered of a sufficiently sacred character as to engage a woman's attention to the exclusion of any other religious duties which must be performed.[1]

In modern times women are more involved in the synagogue, though rarely in a decision-making capacity. They attend the services, form women's committees concerned with decorating the synagogue, fund-raising and arranging social events and they often teach at the Cheder and help to organise the clubs. In the sixties, attendance at synagogue and Cheder were regular social events for both girls and boys, and from adolescence both were equally likely to become involved in the synagogue youth clubs. Since these clubs were very much part of the synagogue and evolved from the earlier, less formal socialising, they were, not surprisingly, rather conservative in outlook.

I remember going to youth clubs and feeling uncomfortable and unreal. I was failing in the main aim of the whole thing – to get off with a boy. Activities at the clubs reflected adult values, with discos, discussion groups, theatre outings and fund-raising events and at some clubs, sports and rambling. Traditional religious values, basic social structures and male and female roles were rarely questioned. Ideas and activities which could cause conflict with parents were avoided. On the whole, girls were encouraged to be passive and decorative – you sat around waiting to be asked to dance. A girl who couldn't get a boyfriend tended to feel pretty inadequate. I have never felt terribly comfortable dressed up and always looked ludicrous in make-up – to myself, at any rate. I was never impressed with boys to whom these things mattered. Most girls were preparing for marriage rather than a career and had low social ambitions. Some went to university but more would aim for secretarial courses, early marriage and a lifestyle similar to that of their parents. Overall the main attraction of the synagogue youth club was to find a nice boy.

It took quite a while for me to realise that there was an alternative. It was my parents who pointed me in the direction of Habonim, one of the youth movements, and who encouraged me to start going there. Habonim was the largest and best known of the youth movements active in England at the time, which is perhaps why my parents chose it.

The youth movements were quite different from the synagogue youth clubs. While the clubs reflected and upheld traditional Jewish values and lifestyle, the youth movements in their origins and modern-day aims sought to change them. The values of the movements were those of socialism and Zionism, rather than religion, and while the power of the synagogue lay mainly with the elders of the community, the growth and direction of the Zionist movement has depended on its young people. Its roots lie in nineteenth-century Russia, where the end of serfdom and some relaxation of anti-Semitic legislation led Jews to move out of the Pale of Settlement, the ghettoes where they had been obliged to live and into the towns and cities of Eastern Europe. Many became involved in socialist political activity and formed a high proportion of the membership of revolutionary parties. From these socialist movements grew the idea of creating a national home for the Jews in Palestine. Zionism was seen as the only long-term solution to the oppression of Jews, and from 1880 emigration from Eastern Europe to Palestine began. The early settlers established collective agricultural communities run on socialist principles. Meanwhile Zionism was making its way through Europe, and losing *en route* some of its revolutionary spirit, so that, for instance, the First World Zionist Congress in Basel in 1897 included no Jews from Palestine and opposed the growth of cooperative settlements. The present-day youth movements, such as Dror, Hashomen Hatza'ir and Habonim, have evolved from these Zionist movements in Europe. They have in common the Zionist ideal of a Jewish home-land but vary in their commitment to socialism. Each movement is linked to a particular kibbutz movement and to a political party in Israel.

I belonged to Habonim for several years. Most people there were quite scathing about 'the bourgeois youth club scene' and at the time when I went to both, I was embarrassed if anyone from Habonim saw me dressed up to go to a club. Although, in Habonim, people did pair off, it seemed acceptable not to be in a couple. A girl could feel more of a person there and less of an object in a cattle market. The youth movements at their best encapsulated ideals essential to Judaism and often masked in ritualistic religion: ideals of self development, social responsibility and working for a better community. We talked about and supported CND and the anti-apartheid movement. We listened to Bob Dylan and Joan Baez. I felt a strong Jewish cultural identity grow through Habonim. This came partly from learning modern Hebrew. We used many everyday words such as *mitbach* for the kitchen and *sifria* for the library. It came also from an awareness of recent Jewish history, including the establishment of the state of Israel and from learning Israeli songs and dances. Almost all the dances were in a circle or formation rather than in couples, so everyone could be involved and girls weren't left waiting to be asked to dance. At celebrations we sang Israeli songs and danced Israeli dances.

For the first few years in the movment it felt as if the division between boys' and girls' roles had been broken down. We modelled ourselves on Israel's revolutionary pioneers. There seemed no reason why boys and girls alike could not take part in political discussion, put up a tent, run groups for the younger children and manage the Moadon (the youth centre). Outdoor skills like camping and walking were encouraged and both the girls and boys took part. The twice-yearly camps were a main focus of activity and reinforced our sense of unity with Jews from other parts of England, from Europe and from Israel. There was a freer attitude to sex though no particular pressure to sleep with your boyfriend. Girls gained the impression that women were more than just ornamental and nurturing. Smart clothes were positively discouraged and girls usually left their hair long and rarely wore make-up. It was not just that we did not dress up. We rarely even wore a home-made skirt, which would have been cheaper than jeans. The norm of 'jeans and a movement shirt' symbolised an attempt at equality for girls and boys. The youth movements each had their own distinctive shirt which was the same for girls and boys. Habonim's was a blue smock-shaped shirt, the larger and more faded the better, with red string ties at the neck.

Habonim did not reject religion outright, but it did not give it a central role. Some observances were retained partly for their value in strengthening our Jewish identity and partly so that children from more orthodox homes would not be at a disadvantage. The food was always kosher, for example. There was an emphasis on festivals that helped us to relate to recent Jewish history and to the experience of other oppressed groups. Passover was particularly important. It is the celebration of escape from slavery in Egypt and the crossing of the desert to freedom in Palestine. We held our own Seder night (Passover meal) and, instead of reciting the story of Moses and Pharoah as we would at home, we read accounts of Jews in the concentration camps and of Black people in South Africa and other freedom struggles.

Once I was established in Habonim, I absorbed the movement's rejection of the surrounding teenage culture, but I am not sure why I chose to stay in the first place. It was my first experience of questioning the status quo. For many people the confidence gained from taking up the challenge led to family conflict when parental values were questioned. This was more the case for Rachel, my younger sister, than for me. Early on, having learned about it from me, she made a firm choice in favour of the movement. She was quite well established there before she had even tried the youth club scene. Becoming accepted in Habonim could take as much as a year. You had to go to Israeli dancing, modern Hebrew classes and weekend and summer camps as well as the regular weekly meetings, and also present yourself as an interesting and lively person. It was both demanding and challenging. To our parents, our requests to go to mixed camps or to be out two or three evenings a week were extreme enough. We chose to look a right sight into the bargain.

Initially, Habonim gave girls a strong sense of equality. We saw older girls in positions of responsibility, leading groups, running camps and having equality on a social and political level. But as we got older and could see more behind the scenes, this ideal seemed to tarnish. At seventeen, my sister went to live in the Bayit, a communal house of the movement, where most people were working in the movement and preparing for eventual emigration to Israel. She untypically was studying for her A-levels. The women in the Bayit gradually seemed to take on more and more of the housework. There was a rota for cleaning, but since women seemed to care more about the place being kept clean, they were usually the ones who got it done. The same went for cooking.

There was a rota, but it was generally accepted that the women cooked better and after a while they got tired of eating burnt, half-cooked food and would end up doing a larger share.

The age of seventeen or so seemed a turning point for most people in the movement. It was the end of seeing it primarily as social life and the beginning of commitment. Groups were formed to go on Hachshara – a year's stay in Israel, working and studying on kibbutz with some time in the army. The group would then return to England, some to go to college, some to do movement work, and then wait to go back to Israel to settle on kibbutz with the same group. Some inequality began to show itself here, too. More boys than girls went on Hachshara, perhaps because parents were more likely to be anxious about a daughter leaving home and travelling abroad. Rachel had had a boyfriend in Habonim since she was fifteen. They spent the summer before she moved into the Bayit working together on a kibbutz. She was already finding it hard to remain a convinced Zionist, or to believe that Israel was where she belonged. The problem, as she saw it, was that if nation-alism was wrong in general how could Zionism be right? Her boyfriend planned to go on Aliya (to emigrate to Israel) and as she was 'in love' with him she wanted to be persuaded back into believing in the same ideals. But she felt that in Israel there would be no slot that she could easily fit into. The choices of work on kibbutz would be kitchen, laundry or childcare (though a few men did work with children) or maybe the garden. She saw none of the kibbutz women doing agricultural work, even though this was quite a young kibbutz. After the trip to Israel she felt somehow that they would split up before he emigrated and in fact they did, a year later.

When a group got together to go on Aliya, there were far fewer single women than single men. It often seemed that the women had gone along with the politics but had not become fully committed. It was very noticeable that when a couple planning to go on Aliya split up, the man generally went ahead anyway and the woman stayed behind. It was sad to discover that women had just tagged along all that time. I had never been a sufficiently adventurous teenager to think of Aliya. Just moving seven miles south of Kilburn to Stockwell at the age of twenty-two seemed quite a grand undertaking and a major departure from the parental home. However, at fourteen, Rachel's life plan had been Hachshara, then emigration, so leaving the movement at seventeen meant a huge rethinking of her life. Nevertheless, Habonim has had a strong influence on both of us and we learned a great deal from it. Rachel found that the time she had spent thinking about why she had rejected it helped her work out what she actually wanted. I found that at seventeen, almost unnoticeably, I grew out of any part I could comfortably play within the movement, and moved into the conventional preoccupations of finding a job and applying for college. At work in a factory, then in a hospital, I moved for the first time in a completely non-Jewish social sphere. Then going to college for three years I did again seek a Jewish network, though at the same time I was almost compulsively seeking all sorts of other contacts. I became involved, simultaneously in the college Jewish society, the Christian peace movement and various leftish political groups concerned with anti-racist work, community projects and the Third World.

Habonim did give me the experience of questioning the social structure, though more from a socialist than a feminist viewpoint. It was less sexist than other social settings, but could lead to the view that if equality was possible here, what was all the fuss about. It taught me to respond to oppression with organisation, pride in my identity and the development of a separate community. Ultimately the solution seemed to be 'we can only be ourselves in our own country'. There seem to be parallels for the women's movement, but with separatism as the logical conclusion.

The synagogue, on the other hand, reflected traditional family values. It too gave us the concept of being a separate, oppressed group, but the response seemed rather more passive. There was tacit support for Israel, largely through fund-raising, and emphasis on upholding religious traditions as the only way to preserve the Jewish race. Even if we were oppressed, we were still the Chosen People. The message to women seemed to be 'a good marriage is hard work, motherhood is noble and a sacrifice'. The implicit aim of the synagogue was the development of a separate, parallel community without standing out as too different from everyone else, while the explicit aim of the youth movement was Aliya, *not* integration. If either path were truly followed to its goal, it would be very hard to be a feminist. In both, feminist consciousness seemed to start at the points where a woman began to question what was being offered.

Up to now, both my sister and I have remained single, stroppy women who have, perhaps 'selfishly', taken up the benefits of education without solidly committing ourselves to a career, though we have worked hard intermittently within teaching and social work respectively. Eight years apart in age, and coming into contact with the youth movements and then the women's movement at rather different stages, it was a surprise to both of us to find out at how many points our experiences and ideas overlapped. Many aspects of the women's movement which seemed to be very new to our friends, in particular the rejection of a decorative or passive role, had already been part of our experience in Habonim. Such a change would have been harder if we had only been immersed in the religious side of being Jewish. But the women's movement has brought us many new things. In Judaism, a woman often feels forced into a community of women, for instance in sitting apart in the synagogue, but she experiences the community as an inferior one. In the youth movement there tended to be a denial of any difference between men and women and so gave us neither positive nor negative experiences of identifying with other women. The challenge of the women's movement, for me, was that it emphasised the positive identification with women, the positive choice to be part of a community of women.

Poems

Margaret Wright

I still find it difficult to say her name. Writing it now, 'Alison', I am able to distance myself enough to set down what lies below.

She had just begun to name her world and so help me to rediscover mine when she fell ill. The illness took both word and world away from her. Grief-stricken and afraid, I sat still, gave complete attention to her, and carried her through to wherever it was that she was going. She never failed to let me know what to do. We had long enough to take leave.

Although the doctors in the community kept reassuring me and telling me she would get better, in the hospital they found it hard to believe that she had ever been a normal child. I watched a nurse carry her away into intensive care down a long corridor, wrapped in a blanket, her legs dangling. A little while later her clothes were brought back to me in a large white plastic bag. They diagnosed her illness straight away and began treatment. I had been right about her all the time. She was expected to die during the night; but in the morning she was still alive. By now, in this environment, she had become a 'problem' to be objectively discussed. A day later, certain that she would not make a satisfactory recovery, they put it to us that the antibiotics and feeding tube should be withdrawn. She would then starve to death under sedation. This, they said, could take quite a long time, maybe nine days.

Anger rose above fear. I damned them for their tidy ending and made the decision I would be able to live with for the rest of my life.

The feeding tube, bypassing her right to die, caused me great anguish. Women friends came. We never left her, taking it in turns to massage her face to lessen the spasm so that she could eat. The feeding tube was withdrawn and she ate earlier than had been expected. I took her back home as soon as possible as I felt the hospital were ambivalent about her survival. They were coping with failure in their terms.

If I moved Alison she screamed and would not stop. Soon however I discovered that holding her upside down over my knees brought her peace. She would fall asleep, vertical, with me holding her bent arms. Children came to play with her older brother and sister. They taught me a lot. A girl came one day when I was holding her upside down, asleep.

'Does she dream?' she asked.

'I think she probably does,' I said.

'Well,' said the child, 'I hope she dreams of playing then.'

The poems surfaced as I became able to open up to the depths of my grief. The solicitor, acting on her behalf, shouts at me in exasperation, 'Mrs Wright, if you speak from your experience, the judge will stop listening to you.'[1]

But you are listening.

My poems, dedicated to the daughter who has gone beyond my understanding, speak from that experience and are written for you.

So the Icelandic Poppy . . .
(for Alison at five)

She was in haste
To be born
Opened and shone
The precious summer of an arctic plant.

The winter's long

In my heart
The scattered seeds
lie strewn.

Night Passage
(Alison screamed for six months, she screamed all night)

Last night a great storm rose
My boat, her ballast gone
Spun in the giant sea
Out of control, alone.

Blind waves of salt-grief lashed
As her cries rose and fell
Within my ringing skull.

But daylight found us safe
Flung up beyond the foam
Past the high water line

My tears had brought us home.

Newbrough

Revealing October!
Leaves flame; then fall.
Trees new sculpted
Glint or drip
Baring first trunk
Next the structure of branch.

Come closer now.
In the grooved bark finger the North
That leaves a green stain.
The weather's wayward.
At evening with the curtains drawn
Listen.
Is that the dry leaves' rustle
Or else that crackle-fire-in-the-roof that's hail?

So taking leave strips bare
Uncovering layer on layer
Till, in that close thicket which hides fear
I watch the stricken ram appear.
But now, released,
He flies down the valley in the rising mist.
See here, etched on my stinging hand
Thin lines of bright red droplets stand.

Driftwood

Even spring's tides
Cannot retrieve
This blond-washed wood
Thrown up the bay so far
By winter's storms.
We struggle now

To lug it home
To burn.
No use as kindling
Once it catches on
Salt spits
As planks shift
Red-bellied on the coals
Remembering some sea change
Weathered how long
In moon-drenched waters.
Shadows jerk
Pitch-pine still fragrant
Flares.
My hearth sings
With its unlikely harvest.

Aspects of the Great Mother

'Tell them . . . as I dying live,
so they dying will live again' . . . These are the words of the Ever-lasting and Everchanging Moon-Mother. I believe that the ancient Women cultures are not just of the past . . . but that they co-exist with us now. That past, present and future co-exist in another dimension/reality and that we tune into those women and 'hear' them.

I felt many times, long ago, that I was in direct communication with the ancient, powerful and creative women and that from them came the guidance and the images/dreams/incantations of my paintings.

To me, feminism means the rebirth of the Goddess . . . she who is our infinite Self. For this to happen we must also act politically to throw off the shackles of capitalist and imperialist patriarchy . . . so as to free ourselves and to set free again our Mother, the Earth.

We are slowly beginning to regain some of our ancient menstrual, psychic, bisexual, visionary collective Womanpowers.

It is slowly beginning to hum within us . . . deep, deep within . . . slowly, slowly we are reawakening . . .

Monica Sjöö, Candlemas in Cymru, Wales, 1982

The Woman Who Wanted to Be a Hero

Michèle Roberts

I am full of fear when I sit down to try to write about my spirituality. I am a complete beginner in the spiritual life. It's only fairly recently that I've begun to value spirituality again, after a long time of not listening to its call, burying my need for it. I have not got the wisdom born of steady growth over a long period; I'm aware of my ignorance and inexperience, and what has been up to now my lack of serious commitment. I've never learned to meditate properly, for example. All I can offer you is the story of how I arrived at beginning to want to let spirituality grow in me; it's dishonest to suggest I can offer anything more.

It is very difficult to write about spirituality, anyway, for spiritual experiences occur in a realm beyond language. Those who try to communicate them run into problems immediately. One of the mystical works which had a strong influence on me in my teens was the fourteenth-century *Cloud of Unknowing*, whose author grapples at length with this problem of how to express the inexpressible, how to name in human terms experiences which carry us out of the human concepts of time and place. He ends up using what he calls the Negative Way: we name and experience God through what he is not, constantly reminding ourselves of his difference from us. This induces a humble longing for him, the necessary condition of receptivity to him. So the author goes as far towards emptying out language as he can. Other medieval writers adopt and adapt the language of formalised erotic love, describing God's union with the soul in the terms of physical union, the sensations of heat, sweetness and light. But none of these writers (here I am talking only of the Christian tradition) ever expresses the belief that language is a sufficient tool for describing religious experience. Many people, of course, consider that it is arrogant and exhibitionistic even to try.

The history of my own spirituality necessarily includes the history of my struggle first to name and then to integrate what have felt like warring, separate parts of myself: body, soul, intellect, emotions. These conflicts name me as a child of the Judaeo-Christian tradition, which, to put it very crudely, operates within a dualistic and hierarchical system of concepts: soul is better than body; be guided by intellect, not by intuition. And since this tradition has designated and denigrated women as bodies and as bundles of emotions rather than as possessors also of souls and minds (traditionally reserved for men), my struggle has concentrated on validating the body and the emotions, exploring sexuality and emotion in order to assert their beauty and worth. Now, I am able to say that I am both woman and whole, whole *because* woman. This involves reclaiming my soul too. The journey to this point has been long and very painful. The truest record and explanation of it is contained in my novels and poems. I became a writer through sheer necessity. I desperately needed to describe experience in order not to be overwhelmed by it, to name the conflicts inside myself, to imagine solutions to them, to create images and meanings of femininity that were not divisive, damaging, silencing.

I was born in May 1949, twenty minutes after my twin sister Marguerite. I have an older sister, Jacqueline, and a younger brother, Andrew. My mother is French, and a devout Catholic in the French way: unsentimental, unawed by priestly authority, full of practical kindness. She has always been a powerful woman in the local church community. My father is English and Protestant; his religion is entwined with the social life in the village where he and my mother live, and means more and more to him, I think, as he gets older. My mother had to promise at her wedding to raise her children as Catholics, and she kept this promise; I remember her fighting my father and insisting that we be sent to convent school. We were.

Nowadays I make a distinction between spiritual experience (which is individual and anti-authority, aimed at creating a guiding principle within the self) and religious institutions (which depend on collective obedience to an exterior authority), but as it was the Catholic Church which first offered me the language of spirituality, I need to talk about it.

Catholicism felt physically part of me from birth onwards (that's what I see now, looking back), as integral as the blood in my veins, passed on to me by my mother like milk. Catholicism was language itself: a complete system of images, and such a rich one, within which to live and name the world. It was literally my mother tongue: my mother spoke to us in French, and we grew up bilingual. Catholicism defined my mother's autonomy in her marriage; she gave up many aspects of being French through coming to live in England, but she held on to her religion always. As children, we spent long summer holidays at our grandparents' home in the Normandy countryside within a culture where religion was as necessary as breathing, inextricably woven into personal and social life. The church bells divided the day not just into hours but into the moments of the liturgy: the Angelus, Mass, the Office. The festivals divided the year into a vibrant chronology. Catholicism made utter sense to me as a religion for country people: its imagery was rooted in the daily events of farming life, and its major feasts marked and celebrated the specific achievements of the turning seasons. I knew intuitively, somehow, that the Catholic feasts overlaid the older, pagan cele-brations and rituals around birth, sexuality, death.

Spirituality wasn't confined within the walls of churches. Early childhood was a time of unselfconscious identification with the natural world: I rarely felt separate from it. My skin, the boundary between me and trees, clouds, rocks, seemed easily to dissolve, and I only knew that I was human and different when I found myself crying at things that were so beautiful they were almost painful: electric blue twilights, the stars, the sea. These experiences diminished as I grew older and built up defences against feeling. I remember distinctly one experience, when I was about ten, when I felt I met God. I was exploring Harrow-on-the-Hill, and came into a Quaker graveyard that was a garden, full of bees and grass and flowering bushes. The peace in that place was tangible. I felt someone touching my face very gently, as though to say: be still; be healed. I had a similar experience last winter, staying in the Lake District in a house once occupied by a community of Quaker women. When I was twenty-three and living in South-East Asia, I smoked Buddha grass and ate hallucinogenic mushrooms and recaptured and re-experienced the mystical way of being of child-hood: complete loss of ego, complete merging with the natural world around me, a profound understanding that language was only a convention with its names that divided *me* from, say, a rock or a tree. I saw how we were the same, how the dance of atoms was in all of us, how we were all, people and plants and mountains and animals, connected to one another in the shimmy of continual change. When I was a child, I knew that everything was in a state of continual connection and movement, but I repressed that knowledge during my adolescence, and again in my mid- to late twenties, and suffered accordingly.

I can't remember a time during childhood and adolescence when I didn't pray. God was my constant companion to whom I talked all the time, pouring out praise, love, yearning. Some of these silent cries were really directed, I think, at my mother, from whom I felt I had been separated too soon: being a twin, I couldn't have her undivided attention (of course no child can, really) and she soon had another baby, my brother, to care for as well. So my mother was for me the powerful, queenly Virgin Mary, the land flowing with milk and honey, and I was the Israelites in exile, yearning to be reunited with her. It was to her that I dedicated the May altars that I built in the hall at home, and to her that I prayed for forgiveness. My anger at my loss of her was, I was convinced, a terrible sin, akin to murder. Guilt encouraged me to make reparation: the mother whom I damaged in fantasy could be magically restored with offerings of flowers, candles, poems and prayers.

I don't think that I thought then of God as masculine, despite the convention of addressing *him* as *he*. God functioned as a perfect, ever-present mother, yet at the same time was pure spirit, unsexed. The lack of gender felt comfortable. I had problems with my own gender, could not and did not want to identify with my mother as a feminine being. Puberty, which marked me as female in a way I'd never had to face before, was a terrible shock, destroying my androgynous self-image and identification with plants and animals and reducing me, I felt, to an identity that was partial, negative, and terrifying, because it pointed me towards a certain and limiting fate; I felt that freedom and choice were removed from women.

I decided, even before puberty, to become a nun. I remember at nine years old solemnly writing in my diary that I intended to serve Jesus by becoming a missionary in the Congo, which seemed to me a splendid destiny. My twin read out this passage to friends at primary school, who thought it was very funny. Really, I think, I wanted to become a monk; I learned early on that men had more status. It would be crudely reductionist, and dismissive of spirituality as an autonomous force, to suggest here that I was motivated solely by adolescent fear of sexuality and motherhood, but that certainly played a part in my decision. I did see the convent as a retreat from the frightening world of the sexual double standard (which was well inculcated by the nuns at school) and from the odiously submissive images of femininity purveyed by the culture. I did want to escape my body, which I hated: the breasts and menstrual blood which arrived when I was only ten, the spots and frizzy hair and plumpness which made me despair of ever measuring up as conventionally pretty. Wanting to become a nun *was* a way of escaping the implications of my gender, but it also represented a way of hanging onto some sort of a spiritual life, some autonomy, power and respect. I divided the animal and the spiritual very sharply, and felt I had to choose between one or the other. I was also arrogant and ambitious, wanting to be perfect, and the church taught that the religious vocation was the highest. It was like trying to be top of the class, something else I went in for.

Many of the nuns who educated me were sentimental, immature, and wilfully ignorant (just as I was); a couple of shining exceptions were tough intellectuals, honest and mature people (such as I longed to be) who were clearly not in retreat from anything, although both later left the convent. These two nuns offered me an image of female power and autonomy that I could not discern anywhere else (I couldn't, at that age, as I've said, admire it in my mother). Years later, when I started reading books by Jungian feminists, I discovered the archetype of the virgin, the woman who exists for herself, Diana the huntress, who is both chaste and sexual, mother of many children but belonging to no man. I can see now what I was groping towards. Catholicism, of course, divides the idea of virginity (autonomy, belonging to yourself) from sexuality, and sexuality from motherhood, so no wonder I was confused. I ended up trying to renounce not just sexuality (pre-marital sex was in any case totally taboo) but also emotion. This amounted to renouncing my self, my femininity. I was rather like one of those nymphs in Greek legend, who, to escape male pursuit, changes herself into a tree. There is some power in that. The church fathers named women as part of nature, not simply to be interacted with, but as something to be feared, controlled and exploited. Very well then, I'd go one step further, cease to be a woman at all, disappear into nature.

I poured all my passion and energy into going to Mass, praying, performing acts of mortification to gain forgiveness for my sins, which I felt were legion because I disliked myself so much. I sincerely wanted to be holy and to love others more than myself, but I was a prig, ostentatiously helpful at home and at school, walking along the school corridors close to the walls with a down-cast expression, the way the nuns did (my twin told me I looked revoltingly smug). I persuaded myself into appropriate feelings: for example, I convinced myself that school religious retreats were profound religious experiences, which they were not, and that confirmation imparted something beautiful to me, whereas in fact I felt nothing. At the same time I wished I wasn't such a prim, awkward wallflower at the dances my more extrovert twin dragged me to, wrote poetry in secret and yearned to enter the decadent, wicked world of Baudelaire and Mallarmé, could not repress my sexual feelings when I read the poems of John Donne or listened to Bach (I remember my father finding me prone on the floor in ecstasy one day and rushing off to fetch my mother, calling to her that I was ill).

In the sixth form, I read all the modern Dutch and German theologians I could lay my hands on, the thinkers who were rock-ing the boat. I also discovered Theilhard de Chardin and Thomas Merton; it was the latter's description of his spiritual quest that led him to a Trappist monastery and thence, without leaving the monastery, to Zen Buddhism, that confirmed my own longing to be a contemplative nun. But I was also discovering that I wanted to go to university and develop intellectually, to sample all that the world had to offer. I told myself that I'd give it all up later; the renunciation would be all the grander if I tasted the sweets of life first. When Sister Bonaventure, the school librarian, told me one day that Oxford was a den of iniquity (she really used those words) and that she really knew because she'd been there, I knew that I wanted to go too. And because I had concentrated on becoming an intellectual, rejecting traditional femininity and social life and spending hours in libraries, I had enough eclectic, eccentric knowledge and enthusiasm to pass the entrance exam.

Oxford meant trendy Dominicans conducting Mass to the sound of guitar music and the scent of joss sticks; it meant a women's college with its community of serious scholars whom I gladly assumed were all either celibate or lesbian; it meant creating friendships with women which I hope will last life long; it meant being a brain by day and a sexpot (a virginal one) by night and miserably feeling I failed at both; it meant discovering that upper-class undergraduates mostly thought that middle-class ones were despicable and drab; it meant encountering feminism for the first time, and for the first time feeling that I was not mad, for the first time feeling that my conflicts had perhaps something to do with the kind of culture I lived in and its ambivalent attitude towards women. I chose to specialise in medieval English literature, so that I could plunge into reading religious poetry and mystical literature in depth. I loved the work not just for its intellectual sake but for the spiritual meanings embodied in the texts I studied. I was a child of Catholicism, and here I was being allowed to inherit the messages of the mystics, spend hours thinking and writing about them. I remember one summer going walking in Burgundy, and visiting the exquisite Romanesque church at Vezelay which was preserved in all its original beauty and austerity of white stone, and feeling overwhelmed by the ancient messages emanating from the stone carvings on the columns and doors, images I could read off because of their roots in my Catholic childhood and now in my studies. Attending Mass in that place resonating with the history of pilgrimage and monasticism aroused all my old yearnings, mixed with uneasiness: I desperately wanted to believe in God still, to reach out beyond myself, but was less convinced now that I did believe in the Catholic God.

I almost stayed on at Oxford to pursue research on a woman fourteenth-century mystic I'd begun to read, Magda of Thagdeburg, but was pulled towards London by curiosity for the big city, the capital, the desire to be in what I imagined was the heart of things. From being rather nun-like (despite forays into dope smoking, drinking, friendships with bohemians and revolutionaries, all the usual student stuff) I experimented with the opposite, joining a libertarian commune where rooms, clothes and possessions were held in common and sexual freedom was encouraged. Convent-like in its way, with unspoken rules and group confession. It did me a lot of good, though in a violent way, shaking me up, turning my psyche inside out. Along with feminism, I embraced Marxism, with all the intolerance and enthusiasm of the ex-Catholic, for such I now was. My religious beliefs dropped away with no great struggle on my part; in fact I simply exchanged one orthodoxy for another. I also attempted radical surgery on myself, sought to excise memory and the past, my unconscious, the system of images which had formed me, the culture and class I came from. I scorned spirituality and what went on inside me, seeing it as irrevocably connected with the Catholic Church's historical role in aiding the state's oppression of the poor. I became overwhelmed at this time by the suffering in the world, the exploitative difference between the Third World and ourselves, the genocide of the Vietnam War. Spirituality seemed to be petit-bourgeois self-indulgence, a private refuge from mass horror. I was completely intolerant of friends who sought gurus and enlightenment and vanished to the ashram in Poona, seeing it as a cop-out for the rich. But I was increasingly unhappy in the commune, and ran away by getting a job with the British Council in Thailand, attempting to cut off, be born again in some way, reject my old self and magically create a new one.

My Thai friends were all Buddhists, but my anti-religious stance kept me from learning anything from them; I did not understand what seemed to me their quietism and fatalism in the face of death and suffering. I noted *en passant* that Thai Buddhism denies women souls; we have to wait for a higher rebirth. Falling apart under the contradiction of being well off, white, implicitly supporting American imperialism through working for the British Council, and yet calling myself a Marxist, I decided to return to England, clear that I had to sort myself out in my own country. I parted from the man I loved in order to return. He wanted to marry me and have children, and was prepared to leave his wife for me. I rejected him, driven by guilt and conflicts I couldn't explain to him or myself. They expressed themselves in poems whose meanings I only understood later.

I found that there was a novel inside me demanding to come out. I began it on the bus coming back from a visit to my parents. I had a pain-filled row with my mother in which I reproached her bitterly for a lack in myself I could not name. Hurt and puzzled, she repeated her conviction that I was mad. I was certainly ill, trampling down both my sexuality and my spirituality, the only way I felt I could survive. I sat in the bus and scribbled on the back of an envelope: 'There is a dead nun in the school chapel.' It was a tug on my line. Over the next four years, I began to reel in my catch, exploring, with a lot of fear, the connections I found I made between Catholicism, sexuality, repression, mothers and daughters. I had no idea what I would find floating up from my unconscious, and was terrified of monsters emerging. The love and encouragement of men and women friends kept me going, as well as my own conviction that somehow this was healing work, a way of putting the pieces of me back together again. *A Piece of the Night* came out in 1978. Above the body of the dead nun, the sexually and spiritually repressed woman, it resurrects the modern lesbian feminist, the fierce virgin Aphrodite who is also a mother. Lesbianism represented the only way for me to express my femininity, love, creativity.

My heterosexual desires had to be crushed, for I was still unconsciously in the grip of the Catholic divisions of the psyche: allowing men to see me as sexual meant that they would also name me as Other, inhuman, bestial, part of nature to be raped and exploited, lacking a soul. By fleeing from this definition, I accepted it. My feminism at this time contained enormous rage at the wrongs perpetrated on women by men. I identified with the suffering of women everywhere, felt I carried it inside myself. An image of the women's movement that meant a lot to me was that of the goddess Ishtar in her representation as the dark side of the moon, the return of the angry, repressed feminine within patriarchy, the disrespected goddess coming to punish and kill, to bring about a harsh cleansing.

All through the turmoil and struggles of my twenties, good changes were coming about in me, although every moment of change was preceded by depression and mourning, resistance, fear of the unknown. I was still frightened of being open and accepting, yielding to new ideas and ways of thinking. I kept trying to stop time moving me on, to cling rigidly to what I thought I believed and wanted, and to deny the possibility of change. But gradually, I did let myself change. I entered psychotherapy with a wise woman who became a good witch for me, a spiritual guide, slowly drew back towards my mother, went on writing, earned a living, and began to release the buried parts of myself, to try and integrate the split-off archetypes within me.

When I began to have not just friendships but also sexual relationships with men again, I felt guilty at first, feeling that I was betraying the lesbian in myself as well as my lesbian friends. This feeling was underlined by the political divisions that can exist between gay and straight women (though they are not inevitably there), by the way that not just political movements but the culture they mirror/attempt to shatter tries to categorise people in either/or terms. I coped in two linked ways. One was to repress the virgin/lesbian archetype in myself, throwing myself into a rather caricatured femininity (the sort I'd fled from in my teens) that emphasised passivity to an unhelpful extreme. The other was to fall in love with highly masculine, even macho, men, seeing in them the power I did not let myself possess. Of course these men walked all over me. They saw in me the femininity they were frightened of possessing within themselves, and tried to control it by crushing me. Love was impossible because psychic wholeness was being denied on both sides. I was confused and unhappy. Also angry: the repressed, true feminine me rose up complaining.

Driven by these contradictions, I began to write another novel in order to explore gender difference, heterosexuality, to imagine a way of loving men that did not exclude loving women friends. I was surprised, after my years of being a rather dogmatic materialist (elevating first Marxism and then Freudianism into rigid, exclusive authorities), to find myself writing a novel so passionately concerned with the Creation, the Fall, the meaning of original sin, the symbolism of the garden of Eden, Eve as the woman whose intellectual and sexual curiosity (I discovered that these were intertwined) is named by patriarchy as bad. This novel describes and to some extent resolves the conflict I had before starting it about femaleness and creativity. Whereas when I was younger I believed that to be whole and creative and possess a soul I had to deny my femaleness and sexuality, I found I had reached a point in my journey where I could see that my creativity sprang directly from my femaleness, that neither could exist without the other. Creativity entailed exploring my conflicts about being a woman; being a woman meant that I could give birth to a novel.

Again, the ideas of the Jungian feminists, as well as the ongoing experience of psychotherapy, were helpful. I discovered four archetypes which exist within the female psyche: the virgin, the mother, the companion to men, the sibyl. Most of us don't express these aspects of ourselves all at once; we tend to express one or two, to bring out the different aspects of ourselves at different moments in our lives. None is totally separate from the others; they interconnect. For a long while I felt they were all at war in me; I had to spend time recognising them in order to allow them to co-exist. When I looked over poems I'd written some time before, I was surprised to recognise that in a sequence of four poems I had described these four archetypes in terms of patriarchal culture's debased images of women, had recorded my anger at this. Now, I began to recognise the virgin as the lesbian/independent woman who is sexual, free, maternal; the mother as the woman who listens and receives and so conceives not just physical pregnancies but also spiritual ones (conversation, ideas); the companion to men as the vibrantly sexual woman whose business is not necessarily to do with marriage and the bearing and raising of children; the sibyl as the woman who periodically needs to withdraw into what can be seen as depression or even madness but who is in touch with ancient memories, inspiration, who is an artist. This system of imagery helped me to see that sexuality and spirituality can be connected, need not be at war. Also, that a woman can be complete in herself, not just a companion or a shadow to a man, but a distinct being, different to him, in her own right.

The people who have been important and helpful to me around spirituality have mainly been women. My mother, through my darkest times of blaming her for all that went wrong in myself, kept trying to reach me in the only way she could: offering me gifts of food, worrying about my physical well-being. I still yearn for her total approval, but know I'll never get it; my thoughts and feelings upset her too much. I still wish, sometimes, that I could be the daughter she wants and that she could be the mother I want. At the worst, we offend and grieve each other; at the best, we get along by talking about uncontentious aspects of life. In some ways, I am very like her, and this pleases me; on the other hand, there are parts of me that are completely unacceptable to her. We don't meet around religion.

My therapist has listened to me for seven years now, to my complaints, jokes, lies, needs. The experience of being listened to by her enabled me to live. She gave birth to me again, offered me a safe place in which to fight and discover, is encouraging me to become myself fully enough so that I can leave her. I owe her a great deal.

There has also been my English grandmother: tough, funny, rude, realistic, wise, utterly honest. She died two winters ago aged ninety-nine, and I still dream about her and feel her presence. For a year before her death (an accidental fall which broke her hip), she knew that she was dying, and talked to me about it. 'There is no heaven,' she said, 'there is just us together here now.' She was able to accept her own death because she accepted her long, hard life in which she lived and fought with guts, humour and passion. Bereft of the person whose unflagging, often critical love had nourished me all my life, I had to think about death and come to terms with it in a way I had not had to do before. Writing poems about her death helped me to cope with my angry grief, consoled me for the fact that no priestess could sing of her life at her funeral, that no woman could help carry her coffin. I began to understand the poems I wrote as a way of listening, attending, understanding, letting new insights enter me.

There have also been my women friends in the women's movement. In terms specifically of spirituality it was you, Sara, who kept the flame alight during the years I forswore spirituality, or at least tried to. We've argued long and often, you and I, about the value of organised, institutionalised religion. All through the years I was criticising you for being part of the Anglican Church, the establishment, I was grateful (though I never said so) that you took religion so seriously and passionately. For a long time you were the only person I could talk to about it, and yet I often mocked and dismissed your beliefs.

Up until now, then, my spirituality has been very bound up with the fact of being a woman, necessarily so, as I've tried to explain. Psychotherapy enabled me to love again, and also to work. Recovering my sexuality happened alongside discovering that spirituality mattered again. This has meant that I have been able to connect spirituality with activities I once thought were separate from it: eating, conversation, friendship, dancing. I newly understand the sacraments of my childhood as a celebration of these activities. My participation in them is my participation in creation, in the rhythms of creation. Writing poems and novels has become a chief expression of spirituality; and it feels important now to turn outwards and look, through my gendered eyes, at a world dominated by the threat of nuclear war, by the spectre of mass poverty. It feels important to create art around these issues as well as participate in more traditional forms of political action.

For a long time I was scornful of men's spirituality, which I interpreted as the patriarchal (Christian) attempt to deny that man is born of woman and dependent on her, that death is part of the cycle of change, that the body, as part of nature, ages and decays and returns to the earth, part of the atom dance. I saw the Christian God arrogating to himself all the functions of women, and so denying women's part in life and creation. Although the word *God* pops up for me again now, I'm not comfortable with it; it implies something static and transcendent to me. I prefer the term *Dao* as used in the *I Ching* (which I have been throwing and learning from for some years now), a term concerned with movement and perpetual change, a guide for living found within the self, not outside it. The *I Ching* also made me respect the concept of masculinity far more, see it as something positive.

I should explain what I mean by masculine and feminine. I see them not as essential attributes of a given biology, but as images of forms of energy existing within each of us in different ratios. The feminine way tends towards receiving, opening, waxing and waning, relating, uniting. The masculine way tends towards dividing, ordering, separating, naming. Our culture, I think, values the latter more than the former. I've learned, now, to value the feminine within myself. But it's incomplete and insufficient without the masculine. I want to develop this now within myself rather than only see it in men and then do battle with them because I'm denying a part of myself. For years I've criticised men who seem to me to deny their femininity and then fight it in women; but I've been doing the same thing the other way round.

I'm at the beginning again, and can't predict where I shall be going. At the moment I live alone. I enjoy my friends' company immensely, but also need solitude in large amounts. I'd like to feel that I'm travelling towards the stage of being able to live with another person. I know clearly that I want children.

In order to be able to combine, you have to be able to separate. In order to be separate, you have to know how to unite. That's the androgyny I hope I'm moving towards.

A Faith for Feminists?

Angela West

On my thirtieth birthday, I became a Catholic. Eleven months later, my daughter was born and I joined the ranks of Britain's unmarried mothers. When she was two months old, I became a member of a women's group for the first time, and this probably dates the point at which I could call myself a feminist. In the course of a subsequent relationship, my vaguely left-liberal understanding of society was refined into a more thorough-going historical materialist analysis. Meanwhile, I had begun to study theology with the help of the Oxford Dominicans and of my sisters in the Christian feminist movement, especially those in Oxford. And this is more or less what I have been doing ever since.

It is perhaps more than a little strange to begin a feminist auto-biographical sketch with a conversion to Catholicism followed by a 'conversion' to Marxist historical thought. But such has been my experience. Neither of these two 'conversions' mentioned supersede the other but co-exist and cohere in my life, sometimes reinforcing, sometimes challenging each other. I use these two great patriarchal traditions in order to interpret my spiritual concerns within the women's movement; these are expressed in the study and practice of theology in the context of my life and that of my community. To use patriarchal traditions to interpret feminist concerns sounds contradictory. But I experience feminism precisely thus – it forces me to think in and through contradictions. If I didn't attempt to think in this way, I couldn't remain a feminist. To put it more practically, I couldn't remain sane.

In this piece, I want to explore some of the contradictions which I think must be at the base of any feminist hard thinking. And I want also to argue that such hard thinking must inform the spiritual concerns of the women's movement, if these are not to become the means by which women betray both themselves and other women.

It has always been an article of feminist faith that we do our thinking from a basis of personal experience. The emphasis is on understanding gained through personal experience rather than on abstract knowledge developed according to so-called objective criteria. This approach contains an important and profound insight, and one that perhaps more than anything else characterises the style of the women's movement and its politics. Here I wish to present and defend feminist theology as a necessary concern of the women's movement; and I also wish to argue, using my own experience, that there are serious dangers and limitations in basing theology on our own experience.

The first time I really understood what it meant to be a woman, that is to be socially female in this culture, was when I became a mother. As de Beauvoir says, 'One is not born a woman, one becomes one.' In becoming responsible for the life of a totally dependent being, I was brought up sharply against the structures of patriarchy and subjected to them in a way that is not easily imaginable for young, educated, middle-class and economically independent women before it happens to them. The child is powerless, yet she exercises enormous power. Since the mother is identified with the child – I'm not speaking about what is emotionally desirable, but about what is the objective social consequence of childbearing – she becomes, of necessity, a participant in its powerlessness. Thus the child's lack of power delivers the mother over to the

power of the father(s), that is patriarchy. It was in these circumstances, encountering patriarchy for the first time through
motherhood, that I became a feminist. That in itself is a contradiction, for feminism, as it is generally interpreted, is concerned with
the ability of women to transcend the biological and social limitations of femalehood, to become available for that age-old male
project of transcending the limits of existence in a material world
and becoming 'God-like'. As Sartre says, 'Man's fundamental
desire is to be God.' Thus from the outset, I experienced a fairly
fundamental tension in being both a feminist and a child-bearing
woman. I have since noticed that this is a dilemma that is currently
being explored by other feminists.

In my own case, I have found the only way of resolving this
major contradiction has been to locate myself within the space of a
further contradiction, which is apparently even more absurd and
extreme. Christian biblical faith is a tradition based on narratives
that proclaim the unbelievable – that God, believed by the
majority in history, including unbelievers, to represent the
ultimate symbol of male power, reduced Godself to a mere flesh
and blood male, and underwent the complete humiliation of male
power – a fate hardly fit for the Divine, as most people, then and
now, would see it. To proclaim an allegiance to the tradition that
preserves these narratives is to put oneself in the category of being
'religious'; and for most 'secular' feminists and Marxists, it is to
define oneself in a way that is incompatible with being a feminist or
a Marxist. For religion, as many of these critics have adequately
documented, is most frequently the ideological means by which an
oppressive social reality is mystified. The images and values of a
given society are projected into the realm of religious beliefs which
are then used to legitimate the oppressive social structures. For
many feminists, Christianity and Judaism are sexist religions with
a male God and traditions of male leadership that legitimate the
superiority of men in the family and society. Given this analysis,

how can I as a feminist continue to believe in religion? I confess (as one says in the creed) that I do not believe in religion – in as far as religion functions in the way that Marxists and feminists have identified; and I am at one with them in declaring myself an enemy of all religious mystification as it has existed in the Christian church and continues to do so both in that context and elsewhere. This I can do not only as a feminist-materialist but also as a Christian. As a Christian I am an advocate of mystery – more particularly of the central mystery expressed by that ultimate world-historical contradiction that is at the heart of biblical faith, the Incarnation, in which the infinite Creator took on a finite humanity. And I confess it as part of my belief that when and to the extent that Christian faith loses touch with this central contradiction, it breaks faith with itself and becomes a species of religious mystification. It is for me this rootedness in the contradiction of faith that enables me not to collapse all thought onto one or other of the poles of the contradiction but to continue to hold them in tension. And I believe that to be thus rooted in incarnational faith is an intellectual necessity for feminists who wish to think rigorously about the spiritual concerns of the women's movement. I hope to show that this is ultimately the only possible place from which to expose religious mystification in all its forms; these include the ways in which women have been traditionally devalued in patriarchal religion, which feminist theology has taken as its task to expose. But they also include some of the new forms of mystification that feminist spirituality is in danger of producing.

But first we must ask; what is feminist theology and where does it come from? Many feminists have not been entirely happy with the rationalist assumptions that underlie a good deal of contemporary feminism. The dominance of reason is for some too much an aspect of the patriarchal society to which they are opposed. Its discourse provides an inadequate language for that dimension of women's experience which cannot be classed under the heading of rationality, and which has been identified in the context of this book as the spiritual concerns of the women's movement. In search of a language of spirit, some feminists have turned to theology and begun to wonder if God might be the baby who has been thrown out with the patriarchal bath water! In the process of reclaiming the baby, feminist theology has come to birth.

Most of what is published under the title of feminist theology is North American in origin. But recently feminists from this side of the Atlantic have begun to study the methods and conclusions of US feminist theology and in some cases to make their own assessment of it. For example, Mary Condren has recently produced an annotated bibliography of a fairly representative selection of books and articles in the field.[1] In her introduction, she identifies a concern underlying the work: 'to ask basic questions about the actual effects in the real world of theological ideas. The aim is to produce a theology which is liberating at its core, in both method and content.'

The main thrust of feminist theology has been towards overcoming the classical dualism at the heart of western culture, which has been memorably analysed by one of the most well-known feminist theologians, Rosemary Ruether. This dualism, as she shows in her work, is in its primary form a gender dualism whereby women are identified with nature, body and the natural realm, which are all considered to be inferior to the transcendent male spirit. As Mary Condren comments, this has profound political implications for issues such as racism, sexism and class, but these on the whole have not been taken up by feminist theologians other than Ruether. The majority have preferred to concentrate on matters of symbolism, ontology and mythology, and of these by far the most well known is Mary Daly. In her work over the last few years, she has moved in a dramatic progression from a call for reclamation of core Christian symbolism by feminists, to a total rejection – in her latest book

Gyn/Ecology[2] – of all Christian symbolism as irredeemably patriarchal, and its replacement by the notion of God as creative presence of the Verb symbolised in the gynomorphic imagery of the Goddess. Mary Condren describes her work as 'an iconoclastic vision in which theology can only be done in a community of hags [woman-identified women]; men are ontologically incapable of criticising it, and women who do so are automatically identified as "token" women'.

Thus, whereas Christian feminists, like Ruether, have been engaged in the critical re-appropriation of biblical tradition and the attempt to liberate the core of its revelation from sexist structures of interpretation, the 'post-Christians', like Daly, see this as a doomed enterprise. For them, Christian tradition is unreformably patriarchal, and they are concerned instead to replace it with a new mythology based on women's experience, and reflecting their new spiritual consciousness. For many US feminists, this has taken the form of the rediscovery of goddess worship. In Britain, goddess worship is not so prevalent, but there are growing numbers of women who are developing a kind of eclectic spirituality, either 'Christian' in origin or put together from Christian and other religious traditions, but having as its connecting thread the notion of its relevance to or basis in women's experience – in the form of their life cycles, dreams, art, poetry, writings and other products of the female imagination.

What is necessary is a critical appraisal of the notion of 'women's experience', which plays a central role in these new forms of theology and spirituality. There is a discernible tendency in much of this literature to use experience as an essentialist notion – that is, to imply that deep down in every woman under all the layers of false conditioning, there is a pure nugget of unique personal experience; the function of feminism is then to reveal this new womanself in all its pristine glory. It is an attitude which refuses in the last analysis to see experience as that which is constructed in ideology, and therefore falls into the ideological trap. It fails fully to acknowledge that feminism is itself an ideology that seeks to reconstruct personal experience, and is consequently naive about the extent to which it is itself in many ways a product of liberal bourgeois society out of which it has sprung. Thus feminists who treat each woman's experience as unique tend to ignore the degree to which all our personal experience is profoundly conditioned by the dominant ideology of our society. This is true *even when we are taking a critical stand towards that society*. So if as feminists we adhere to the principle of giving equal weight to each woman's expression of her experience, we run the risk of being unable to develop criteria for an effective critique of the society that oppresses women. An aspect of this same problem is identified by Mary Condren in her study; commenting on the 'counter-mythology' of some of the womanspirit groups in the US, she says:

> it may be that particular mythologies can function for particular individuals and small groups, but the question must then be raised as to whether this would merely contribute to the increasing privatisation and individualism of bourgeois culture. It could be argued that this bourgeois culture is a product of patriarchy and its secular manifestation (i.e. that individuals create private functioning world views which sustain them personally, whilst leaving untouched the structural realities which operate in the rest of their alienated lives).

This observation is relevant to what I see as a major contradiction present in feminism as a whole. As we have seen, it is characteristic of feminist ideology that it seeks to re-value women's experience and rescue it from the devaluation it has suffered at the hands of patriarchy. This may seem relatively unproblematic so long as the women whose experience is to be re-valued are members of western bourgeois society. But once one attempts to extend this method to the wider society of women, one is confronted with the fact that the vast majority of women in history and in most contemporary societies tend to see the fulfilment of their lives in the future of their children, and seek to subsume the meaning of their own personal lives in the collective life of the family and culture to which they belong. That is their experience. And I wonder if we as feminists want to be in the position of saying that nearly all women in the world and in history have quite simply got it wrong and we know better. Isn't that to risk devaluing women's experience in just the way that patriarchy has done? The fact that this contradiction has not been adequately commented on by feminists is, I think, a symptom of a lack of historical self-consciousness in our thinking. And it is in this area that I propose that a combination of Marxist analysis and the Christian gospel can serve as a salutary corrective that will restore feminism to its own professed vocation – the liberation of women.

Feminist efforts to reform religious tradition and re-create mythology on the basis of women's experience, have often been, either explicitly or implicitly, part of the attempt to break through that 'gender dualism' in our culture that Ruether has identified. Thus contained within their notion of women's experience is to be found the idea of women's privileged relation to universal nature, which is seen to function as a re-vitalising source for a woman-centred spirituality. This woman/nature connection in feminist spirituality co-exists in a slightly uneasy tension with the classic secular-feminist rejection of the idea that women are to be identi-fied with their biological function. Probably the most extreme forms of this nature-based female spirituality are the goddess cults which attempt to revive the rites of the Great Goddess who is believed by some to underlie the beginnings of all civilisation. The cultists' aim is to return to the old religion of witchcraft, the earth-centred nature-oriented worship that venerated the Goddess as a source of life, and pre-dated the rise of Christianity which, since its inception, has been its traditional foe and ruthless suppressor. In this woman-centred worship they claim to find appropriate symbols of women's strength, power and divine potential that can counter the overwhelmingly male symbolism of God in Christianity, and can create new life-giving rituals as an alternative to the institutional structures of patriarchal religion.

But is latter-day goddess worship actually an authentic feminist alternative to patriarchal religion? Goddess worshippers are one end of the spectrum of a much wider group in bourgeois society including not only feminists and not only women but all those who in one way or another are concerned to 'get back to nature'. Whether it is a matter of being in tune with the rhythms and dictates of one's own body, or of living in harmony with, and respect for, universal nature, there are a great many representatives of this trend. They include health- and whole-food people, bio-rhythm believers, conservationists, Welsh hippy commune dwellers and the like, natural childbirth enthusiasts, naturists, vegetarians, human potentialists, and people (like myself) who count on the privilege of country holidays. All these and more besides could be said to be believers in nature in one or other of her manifestations even if they don't actually worship her personified as the Goddess. By these groups she is believed implicitly or explicitly, to be a benign power, favourable to humans, and in the case of feminists, particularly well disposed towards women who are potentially best able to bear witness to her ways and workings through their intuitive capacities and bodily self-awareness.

About these beliefs, I confess to some scepticism; which is not to say that some of those things identified by nature cultists are not thoroughly good in themselves; still less, to deny that ecological consciousness is a vital concern; but it is to observe that what is missing from the scene is a proper understanding of the class nature of the nature people. Working-class people are not to be found in these movements in any significant numbers; nor are the nations and races of the Third World. The fact is, I suggest that Goddess/ Nature worship, in all its forms, mild and extreme, is in no way an alternative to western bourgeois religion, but simply another manifestation of it. Those who proclaim faith in the goddess Earth and the goodness of nature usually know absolutely nothing of what it means to be immediately dependent on the earth for subsistence or to be subjected to a nature that is fundamentally indifferent to individual human life and survival. We latter-day devotees of the Goddess are the cosseted and over-protected children of a post-industrial technological civilisation, a civilisation that has the power to afford us this protection as a result of the most mammoth and protracted rape of nature that has ever been perpetrated in the history of the earth and its people. Within the safety of the space that capitalist-patriarchy has cleared for us, we can cling nostalgically to this icon of nature that we have set up. And patriarchy is pleased to permit its worship because it represents no threat – it is only the sentimental image of that which we in the West have effectively destroyed. We can afford to go on playing our romantic nature games in comfort and security, while out there the rest of the world is torn apart in hell by the twin ravages of Nature and Man.

An article by Starhawk in *Womanspirit Rising* entitled 'Witchcraft and Women's Culture'[3] seems to me to give this particular game away completely. Talking about the craft rituals of the covens she says: 'They allow us as adults to re-capture the joy of childhood make-believe, of dressing up, of pretending, of play. Magic . . . is not so far removed from the creative fantasy states we enter so easily as children, when our dolls become alive, our bicycles become wild horses, ourselves arctic explorers and queens . . .' While these children of America and western civilisation are happily entering their 'creative fantasy states', children in other parts of the world that have been bullied into submission by the economic might and military machine of the US are existing in a state of abject poverty and misery. They have neither dolls nor bikes nor daily bread sufficient to keep body and soul together. Only the children of the US and the West can afford never to grow up because we are still at play; millions of other children in the world don't grow up either; but that is because they die prematurely of starvation.

When I was a student in the sixties, there was as yet no women's movement; I was one of those liberal-minded Christian souls who espoused radical causes, abjured institutional religion and secretly thought that Christ was an unnecessary and incomprehensible complication of the God-idea. But what really inspired my devotion in those days was not God at all, but Africa. African religion and culture fascinated me for many of the same reasons that women now turn their attention to goddess-worshipping societies and seek to revive their beliefs. My short visit to Africa gave me the sense of a culture that was utterly other than my own, that seemed to be mysteriously in tune with the rhythms of earth and nature. Here too was a kind of warmth and community that was nowhere to be found in the alienated western society that I knew. Later on, as I studied African religion and cosmologies, I felt that here was a kind of wisdom about human social relations that was entirely lacking in my own society. Witchcraft beliefs and practices seemed a sensible way of controlling inevitable social tensions, and living in harmony with one's neighbours and the natural world. I used to shock my middle-class relatives by declaring my belief that Africa was the truly civilised and non-violent society, while we in the West were the savages whose history was nothing but a record of murder and violence.

This love affair with Africa lasted a long time, until finally in the early seventies I returned to Africa and came face to face with the uncomforting realities of a post-colonial society undergoing profound dislocation from its encounter with the western technological world. I began to realise that the Africa I'd worshipped was not only past but in some sense had never actually existed outside my fantasy of it, assembled with the aid of anthropologists' texts and my own youthful yearnings. The reality of twentieth-century post-colonial Africa served to bring me home to myself and revealed me for what I was – an English European marked indelibly by particular cultural assumptions (like privacy and personal autonomy) and formed intellectually in an irrevocably European mould. My former radicalism appeared in its true guise – as a species of idealism which led me, like the missionaries and colonialists before me, to try to make Africa in our own image.

Feminists who seek to base their theology and spirituality on the rehabilitation of nature and what is deemed to be 'naturally human' betray their own social origins and ideological genesis in that period of ascendancy of the bourgeois revolution that has been called the Enlightenment. It was an age that was deeply committed to belief in the natural goodness and progress of man, over and against the Christian doctrine of Sin and the Fall; and it found powerful expression in the work of the eighteenth-century philosopher Jean-Jacques Rousseau, most notably in his philosophical romance *Emile* which has been described as one of the major textbooks of the French Revolution and European Romanticism. For Rousseau, man was naturally good but had been corrupted by society. As André Boutet-Mondel says in his introduction to *Emile*,[4] this was Rousseau's attempt to pursue the question 'how can Natural Man be formed amid the existing corruption? . . . God makes all things good; man meddles with them and they become evil.' For feminists, also wrestling with the problem of man-made corruption, the second part of the formulation takes on a new literalness. It is precisely *man* who has meddled and the result is patriarchy. On this formulation, women then move up into the place of the Noble Savage, Rousseau's imaginary recon-struction of primitive man. And if any feminist feels tempted to subscribe to that vision, let her first read Book V of *Emile* where 'Sophy – or Woman' is introduced as Rousseau's picture of natural woman, the true helpmeet of Emile, the ideal man. I suspect that she will rapidly be convinced that Rousseau's notion of the natural is a thoroughly man-made affair; and will realise with stunning clarity that Man, the product of culture, makes Nature in his own image, just as he makes Woman in his own image and as she suits him. In the same way, I fear, quite a lot of the new feminist spirituality is 'woman-made' in the sense that it is a second-hand version of this eighteenth-century man-made tradi-tion of the Noble Savage. Thus, among goddess worshippers and other feminists who seek to re-evaluate women's historical experi-ence, there has been a renewed interest in the goddess-worshipping societies of the past. But what tends to be ignored by some of these matriarchal enthusiasts is that such societies were often static and cyclical in their orientation, not historically dynamic (as feminists assume themselves to be), and they certainly gave no support to individual autonomy or personal transcendence for any member of the society, still less for women. In some cases they were accompanied by traditions of human sacrifice, young females often being the preferred victim. All this is not surprising if goddess worship is conceived of as the worship of nature; for the power of nature is precisely a power that has no regard for individual life. It is geared to the defence of the species at the expense of the individual.

The notion of nature that can be traced in many areas of feminist theology and spirituality bears out what was suggested earlier; that feminism is not so much a universal truth that has unaccountably not been revealed until modern times but rather a historical phenomenon which like all truth is relative to the particular historical and cultural circumstances of which it is the product.

Feminism is in fact a child of the Enlightenment, and unmistakably reveals its parentage in some of the taken-for-granted values that are the basis of its polemic. These are the values of personal autonomy, rational thought, and the rights and freedom of the individual alongside other individuals. 'Secular' feminism belongs to the rationalist side of this tradition, whereas 'religious' feminism has its source in the notion of Nature, as we saw, and is not so much the opposite of Enlightenment Reason as its complement. They are in fact two sides of the same coin. The bourgeois model of nature is a product of the bourgeois model of Reason. Thus feminist theology finds itself in danger of repeating that classic dualism characteristic of our society, which in good faith it set out to destroy.

This dualism has largely been responsible for the typical forms of western Christianity, and has its origin in the matter/spirit conceptual split that developed with the philosophies of classical culture. They were the product of a society where one section, namely ruling-class males, had achieved personal autonomy and individual rights and could engage in the exercise of reason in its speculative form. This rested on the absolute pre-condition that the rest of the population, women and slaves, could not do so since they were otherwise engaged on the necessary productive and reproductive labour that made possible the freedoms of the ruling male minority. And so it has continued in much the same form, with the working class replacing slaves, and women permanently on the side of matter and unfreedom. Thus constituted, the dominant model of reason in our society has always permitted its beneficiaries to contemplate everything under the sun; only this one fact – the material foundation of reason's freedom – was forbidden them; for once acknowledged, the 'innocence' of patriarchal paradise would be lost forever.

Our conception of rational thought and individual rights is in effect the product of a tradition where reason is a function of male control. For feminists now to locate themselves uncritically within this tradition is by its very nature intensely contradictory. This can be clearly seen in the work of Mary Daly. Several of her critics claim that she has simply reversed the dualism of western culture in favour of women. It is therefore not surprising that Daly is a direct methodological descendant of her male theological forefathers. This is revealed in her essentially idealist understanding of woman. It consists of a series of ethical prescriptions based (as in all idealist thought) on a vision of how the subject (in this case, woman) ought to be, and not on the historical and material reality of woman as she actually is. It is essentially an elitist vision; only the few (and, in a sense, not even the few) can ever hope to live up to the ideal, and they are the ones who are already endowed with the privileges and advantages that fit them to aspire to this ideal/idol created in their own image. Ironically, this description would accurately fit many varieties of patriarchal Christianity as it is practised. It is, I think, no coincidence that Mary Daly rejects the traditions based on Marx and Freud, which are the only ones in modern western thought that seriously question the dominant model of reason that we have inherited and explore its foundation of privilege.

It is clear, to me at least, that in some of our new forms of theology what is really being worshipped – and mystified at the same time – is modern women's experience. And the ultimate meaning of that experience for women as a whole is our subordination to the status quo. Whether we fix our hopes on reason or the goddess, we have not escaped. Like the old pagan god Zeus, the god of patriarchy is capable of changing himself into many forms. If women become suspicious of him in the form of reason, he is not at all averse to masquerading as the goddess. And thus we, like ancient women to their goddess, are still in thrall to the symbols of power that in fact rule our society. As far as human sacrifice is concerned, business is as usual – the only difference being that the former small family business has become a multi-national multi-billion dollar industry.

So how can we rightly interpret the deep sense of ecological disease that many feminists and others feel in these times? How can we witness to the goodness of what is given, and against the existing and impending destruction that we sense not only in the world we inhabit, but in our very selves, the bodies that we are? Not, as I have tried to show, by resorting to one or other form of nature idolatry; for ultimately all such icons contain only the reflection of our distorted nature; they can never be a source of real hope, of salvation for us. For this it is necessary to return to those narratives of the Bible which declare that woman and man were created in the image and likeness of God; which is altogether a different story from the standard patriarchal tale which it has since been translated into, in which God was made in man's self-image of Reason, and Woman and Nature were His/his foil. These narratives are the record of a particular society's understanding of humanity's relationship with creation. The language of nature has been appropriated to express the goodness of that which is given, as opposed to that which is produced by man. But such a language, if it is not to be simply an abstraction of reason, a man-made affair, must be historically mediated. Thus for the authors of these narratives, the relation with nature/creation is contained within the historical relations of their people with their God Yahweh, who is for them, both the Lord of Creation and the Lord of History. Here then we find testimony to the understanding that nature is God-given and good; that it can be destroyed by man; and that the Creator, working in human history amid the ruins of creation, can make nature new out of the dust of our destruction; or to put it in the language of traditional theology, God shall redeem God's people and renew the face of the earth.

To enter into the Hebrew understanding of humanity's relationship to creation, it is necessary to return to the world of the ancient Near East in the first millennium, to the small-scale agricultural society of the Canaanites. According to Ruether theirs was 'the religious culture of the neolithic village where the individual and the community, male and female, earth goddess and sky god were seen in a total perspective of world renewal'. Quite possibly it was not always as idyllic as she makes it sound. In any case, things were set for change; in this period the Canaanites witnessed the arrival of a heterogeneous group of slave refugees from Egypt, with sundry hangers-on, who, by wandering around in the desert for many years, had somehow become possessed by a burning sense of religious nationhood. These people, the Israelites, entered Canaan claiming it as a Promised Land set aside for them by their God Yahweh. To the Canaanites, Yahweh must have seemed very odd as gods go, for he apparently had no use for the goddess or for any other gods – just himself alone, preferring the company of his stiff-necked and rebellious people Israel. This jealous Hebrew God had a most disruptive effect on Canaanite society. The Hebrews took over their new year festivals of renewal of the earth, together with the institution of kingship, but they repressed the feminine divine role integral to the cult, and re-interpreted the old earth celebrations to refer to historical events in the Sinai journey. Thus the festival was severed from its natural base in the renewal of the earth. As Ruether says: 'The messianic hopes of the prophets still looked for a paradisal renewal of the earth and society, but this renewal broke the bounds of possibility and was projected into history as a future event.'

But if Yahweh was apparently the enemy and destroyer of the Canaanite goddess and the worship of nature, it is important to remember that he was never simply the godly guarantor of the new patriarchal state that was ushered in by the march of civilisation in the form of repeated imperial conquest of that part of the Mediterranean. Though the prophets fiercely condemned back-slidings to the polytheistic fertility cults of the Canaanites, they were even more adamantly opposed to the attempts of various Israelite kings to imitate or accommodate the imperial powers that threatened them in the attempt to ensure national survival. Whenever the Israelites turned to protecting or promoting their mini-version of the nation state, a troublesome prophet would appear on the scene castigating all such concerns for national security, reminding them of their desert past when, as a disorganised rabble of ex-slaves, they had no security or salvation whatever outside the faith that their jealous God would somehow see them through to the Promised Land. And whenever they started to become a bit more prosperous and secure, and wanted to show their gratitude to their deity in the proper manner, with festivals and sacrifices, a prophet was at hand to declare that Yahweh was none too interested in religious festivals and holocausts; the stink of sacrifice upset him, it was justice he wanted and his ears were open for the cry of the poor, the widows, the fatherless and those who were hopelessly in debt.

Now these groups were hardly considered to be the most progressive elements of the society of that time any more than they are now; and it was this tendency of the Israelite deity to identify with the marginal elements, the 'wrong class of people', that perhaps had something to do with their conspicuous lack of political success. They never managed to found their own imperial civilisation, but always remained marginal to someone else's, clinging tenaciously to their ethnic identity in an unprogressive fashion. But they did manage to produce one prophet, who despite his political failure, produced such an effect on his followers that it created a stir of unrest right through Graeco-Roman civilisation of those times.

So subversive was the influence of this (no longer) Jewish sect, that the succeeding generations of civilised men were obliged to arrange for its neutralisation by absorbing its teachings into their own philosophical mystique. The resultant cross between Hebrew prophetic teaching and Greek thought was thus spread all over the 'civilised' world and became the matrix of that 'transcendent consciousness' which as Ruether says, 'has literally created the urban earth; both abstract science and revolution are the ultimate products of this will to transcend and dominate the natural world that gave birth to the rebellious spirit'. Feminists, too, feature in the direct line of descent here. They are not the children of the goddess but rather of this same transcendent consciousness and rebellious spirit. And it is this that is also to be found at the heart of modern women's consciousness.

Like a good many other educated western women of the twentieth century, I have spent time exploring the roots of my own female personhood by means of encounter groups, dream therapy, women's groups, community living, contemporary women's literature and much else that is taken by many feminists to be a necessary basis and source of material for creating a feminist theology and spirituality. And it has indeed been very necessary; it has brought me to the place where I now am – the realisation that it is not enough; it has shown me to myself as I am – the product of a particular historical community which has produced contemporary western female experience. But I do not want to go on contemplating that image for ever, to enshrine it like an icon, any more than I want to treat my mirror reflection as a work of art. Narcissism, as we all know, is the way to get drowned. Some years ago I was reading a novel by a contemporary woman novelist whose work I admire and of which I had already read quite a bit. But half way through this novel, I put it down and was never able to finish it. In retrospect, this marks for me the end of a process, the point in which I lost interest in my life as a kind of 'sacred text' and began to turn towards a text that would not so much reflect my experience but relativise it, put it in its historical place by challenging me with the human experience of women – and men – whose experience was utterly other than my own. Only such an encounter could question the historically generated assumptions of my own experience, a questioning that cannot take place within the confines of that experience. And this is how I came to study theology and to pass from regarding the Bible as a rather boring and incomprehensible book to being the sort of text that I shall be happy to have a relationship with for the rest of my life. And just as my feminist beliefs and historical materialist understanding have enabled me to make new sense of the Bible, so in turn this text becomes the basis of a faith that makes possible a further critique of the social and political action I identify with, of the religious tradition in which I am located, and of my feminist commitment.

At one level it has made me sceptical of the transformating grace of sisterhood where this is linked to a falsly romantic feminist utopia; such visions seem to be anodyne, homogenised and tasteless, a typical product of this civilisation and its suburban kitchen heart. But before the sisters accuse me of selling out to the patriarchs, I wish to say that I reject such visions because I believe they betray the real liberation of women. They offer us a new ideal woman (of which we have suffered so many in the past), an ideal that is totally divorced from the actual historical and material reality of the vast majority of women in the world. For these women, individual freedom and personal transcendence must seem like a hollow and deceitful dream; while we are taking wing for a feminist heaven, they remain bound irrevocably to the earth by the weight and power of those powerless infants, whose weight is the weight of the whole human future. Their fate is tied to the fate of the earth, the earth that has been raped, parched, bled and torn apart by patriarchal, capitalist civilisation. These women, and their children will live like that, and they will die like that and when they are dead what difference will it have made to their earthly misery that a few rich women in the western world believed in the social and political emancipation of women and in their right to an authentic religious consciousness? Without ultimate justice, the ultimate liberation for all the powerless, there can never be any true liberation for women.

As a feminist, then, I believe that feminists must locate their lives in the space that women have always lived – that is, in the teeth of patriarchy, and patriarchal systems. As women we have always been pushed to the margins of patriarchal culture, and therefore we should mass in strength and take our stand right there. The only female space that is worth fighting for is that which is wrought out of the male-dominated systems; withdrawing to do theology in the context of the community of hags or the coven of witches is only another version of being relegated to the private domestic sphere that is alloted to all women under patriarchy.

As a feminist I am therefore also a Catholic claiming membership of the universal church and of the communion of saints that it represents. What does that mean? It means being 'in one body' with all those past and present for whom Christ, dying and raised, prefigures the meaning of our ultimate human liberation; it carries with it the obligation of the traditional Christian practices, to pray together, to preach the gospel and to celebrate the eucharist.

To engage in such activities will be seen by most feminists and many others as a profoundly conservative affirmation. Yet our experience as Christian feminists here in Oxford has been the reverse. To take seriously these traditional Christian practices has been to set in motion a process that is subversive of our traditional roles and experience as women. Taking upon ourselves as a community the meaning of the eucharist as a participation in the dying and rising of Christ has served to powerfully reinterpret our experience as the powerless under patriarchy, the childbearers and those whose insights and skills are normally only valued domestically. To preach the gospel means to stand up front and be heard where formerly one sat at the back and made tea. It has meant to read, study and comment on the Bible where formerly theology was reserved for men; it has meant to bring woman's perspective into public moral debate; it has been to discover how praying together (as opposed to discussion, etc.) allows us to cast off the roles and statuses accorded us by patriarchy; it has meant turning again to the Bible and discovering it as an exciting and scandalous book.

The Bible speaks to women precisely because it is *not* a set of instructions about how to get your private passport to heaven. It is the story of an oppressed people who were always getting kicked around by those who were politically more powerful – a people who in the face of their hopeless history preserved a vision of God who would in the endtime redeem them from their earthly humiliation by sending a Messiah to set history right with the coming on earth of God's ultimate justice, and the restoration of the kingdom of Israel.

Unfortunately Yahweh, true to type, didn't quite live up to these expectations. The man who came to announce the coming of God's kingdom and the establishment of his justice was believed by some Jews to be the Messiah. But the mission was a failure – no coming of God in glory, the kingdom of Israel was not restored. The 'messiah' was handed over to the Romans and crucified for political subversion. This was ironic because he really hadn't made a very good job of political subversion. What he had done was to identify himself with the weak and powerless, and he had ended up where all such people end up – as a victim of patriarchy. For what else is patriarchy but the permanent defeat of all those who are materially identified with the powerless – the position of most women throughout history? Women, like the Jews, have been among history's continual victims; their history has focused not so much on the ascent into heaven as the descent into hell – like the hell of the seventeeth-century holocaust of witches or the Jewish holocaust in Auschwitz.

If to be a follower of Christ means to opt in to the historical fate of women and the Jews, who in their right mind would ever take such an option? Isn't such an option madness for feminists who are seeking with the means that are available for perhaps the first time in history to live beyond the traditional historical fate of women?

But this is it; I suggest that the only way women can go beyond our historical fate is to face up to the holocaust society – and venture our lives in its condemnation. The feminist task is precisely to denounce the society that produces the holocaust; all such societies are idolatrous, as the early Christians knew who condemned the idolatry of their society at risk to their lives. And it is here, too, that our witness lies – in the condemnation of the nuclear idolatry of our world, that threatens it with the ultimate blasphemy – the destruction of that world. And for me, it is here that the contradictions of my life experience meet, and are reconciled in the particular and the historical, as they must be, and not in the abstract. As a Catholic, I can take my stand along with other Catholics and condemn nuclear war as 'a crime against God and Humanity' in the words of Catholic social teaching; or as a historical materialist I can recall the words of Marx who prophesied that the only (terrible) alternative to the classless society was 'the mutual ruin of the contending classes'; or as a woman, I can speak from the position I share with all women from time immemorial, even the time of the goddess, the burden of responsibility for the survival of humankind.

This then is what it means to me to be a Christian and a feminist; the Christ event is that alone which can give real meaning to the liberation of women. It is the story of the only scandal that patriarchy couldn't dare to contemplate; the story of God who de-divinised Godself and became a human historical male who turned out to be a complete political failure. It presents God as the ultimate contradiction to the worship of male power, and mocks all gods and goddesses, who are nothing more than this.

In order to show man, and men in particular, that God was not made in the image of man, God became a man, and that manhood was crucified, patriarchal pretensions were put to death. As Paul says: 'For our sake he made him to be sin, who knew no sin' (2 Corinthians 5:21). Christ died on the cross cursed by the patriarchal law; and the law of patriarchy is thus revealed as curse and cursed.

So we may conclude that Christ became Son and not Daughter because the symbol of female power, the goddess, had long since been done to death and needed no further humiliation; and because the daughters of Eve are always and everywhere being brought low through childbearing (or barrenness) and subordinated in the name of the patriarchal God. But in the person of Jesus, God denies the godhead as patriarchal power, and reveals Godself in humanity, in the helpless infant, in the helpless crucified human being. Only from this angle are we in a position to understand the Resurrection, the event in which tortured humanity rose from the dead to show women and men that they are made in the image of God, and not of the male; and that those who have suffered in the body, bleeding, childbearing, crucified, tortured, burned, raped and starved will be raised hereafter.

In the narratives of the New Testament there are no goddesses; there are only human women, active and loving women, suffering in their hope and in their children; bearing the future in their children as women have always done; but bearing the future also in a new way as Christ has done – giving birth through active faith to the life of a new community, the only community in which the liberation of women's bodies is ultimately possible, that is the redeemed community.

For me as a feminist, as much as a Christian, I must affirm my belief in the Resurrection of the body. How can I do otherwise if I am truly committed to the liberation of all womankind, all those living, dead, dying or yet to be born who have been or will be the victims of patriarchal oppression? As José Miranda says:

The negation of the resurrection of the dead is an ideology of the status quo. It is the silencing of the sense of justice that history objectively stirs up. It is to kill the nerve of the real hope of changing this world. The authentically dialectical Marxist and the Christian who remains faithful to the Bible are the last who will be able to renounce the resurrection of the dead.[5]

And to these last I would add: the feminist who really believes in ultimate liberation for all her defeated sisters and their children.

Moontree

The Moon Tree is a recurring theme in ancient imagery, poetry and religious writings. The image of night's light caught in the branches of a tree is an ageless symbol of the Mother's generative powers uniting heaven and earth, a fragment of ordinary visual poetry imbued with her sacred immanent presence.

Meinrad Craighead

Mother Julian's Daughter

Julia Mosse

When my mother Julian saw my Mother God
straddling the heavens, and widening, giving forth the
scream to push the mighty spinning worlds to birth,
she awoke and called it a dream. Big bellied and
tousled, this dried and chaste one saw her God, the
mother of all, heave and pant in creation till the earth
too awoke with a scream. It was the fourth dream.
Julian dreamed always at Whitsuntide: the spirit was
poured on all flesh and the daughters prophesied, saw
visions and wonders. Even the thorn tree – the
suffering tree – and the hole in the stone through
which the river gushed became a benediction. For my
Mother Julian felt herself near death; the dreams were
grace itself, grace to understand and to interpret; grace
yet to perceive the mystery and pleasure in the riddle
while watching the water swirl through the stone. For
sixty years, waking at dawn and bedding at dusk,
counting out the years and the days on her rosary, she
had wondered. Fasting and feasting the mystery had
eluded her. Now grace was come to my Mother Julian.

It was a cold twilight in November. Two figures stood silhouetted against a luminous green slope, poised, undecided. Resolving suddenly, they clutched the heavy folds of their cloaks to themselves and began to descend the hill. The bells echoed back from across the moor. Reaching the narrow cart track at the bottom of the hill, they turned to face each other, again hesitant, reluctant. The taller, stronger figure stretched out an arm and touched her companion on the cheek, then spontaneously pulled her closer. There seemed but one figure at the bottom of the hill; but one became two and the two figures turned away, stepping out east and west along the narrow track. And neither looked back, for one walked towards her shadow and the other walked away. One walked with bright dry eyes, while the taller one walked on weeping.

'Love is all His meaning. Love is all His meaning.' Her steps beat out the words, trying to hammer them into a real place, a deep place in her side. But the images of the past three weeks could not be put aside. Again and again they must be worked through, wept through; and now as she walked east and far away from those three weeks, the fragile covers of her mind parted and the pictures – the bright, real pictures – flickered on and on. Julian calling them, laughing with them. Julian entreating them, blessing them, rebuking them; Julian suffering; Julian dying. The bells. The bells that rang out as they laid her under the shadow of the great rolling moor. Each picture must be held and suffered, each expression repossessed and grieved over. No, not that only . . . for death is a deep still pool into which we all must look; not only our down-turned faces look back, but the strength of our grasp on a brother's, a sister's, a father's hand. All that it seen and all that is unseen; all that is known and all that is unknown is reflected back as we look into the face of a dying woman.

So the young woman stepped on as the night thickened around her. The decaying leaves made the ground soft and damp above the stony track. *Was* the world but a little thing the size of a hazelnut held in the palm of the hand as Julian had been shown it, existing both now and forever because of God's love for it? Sustained, because of love? To her, it was weight, overwhelming weight, but then she had stepped outside a circle that had seemed to enclose only Julian as she died. Julian was held in a hand from which she was rejected. She walked on, picking her way between the pools of rainwater filling the hollowed-out cart tracks, descending further into the valley where a light from a dimly lit window threw out an enfeebled welcome. She had arrived home.

The explanations that must be gone through! The horse cart that had dropped her at the top of the hill so that she could walk the remaining distance and see her companion on her way. Her pale, exhausted face, deeply etched by sleeplessness, her sudden unannounced return home.

'Why?' they wanted to know.

'To start again,' was all that she could answer, 'because Julian was dead.'

'And who was Julian?' they asked. 'Ah, the Anchorite of Norwich,' they nodded sagely. 'The one that sees visions,' they added to themselves.

On a December night, a few days later, she carried a light through the long, cold, stone passages of the house. She carried a light, a book and a pen. Settling herself in a small square room she opened the book and began to read. '. . . Now grace was come to my Mother Julian.' But what next? What else had Julian said of the shewings? The human breast that suckles the child and the breast of our gentle Mother Jesus, tenderly feeding us through the bread and the wine. That, and the stream of blood, and the gouging thorns – a garland of thorns dyed with a stream of blood. The woman sat still and silent for a long time while the flame flickered in the dim room. Finally, bending her head close over the page she began:

'I cannot see God without Julian,' she wrote. 'Her visions were all that I knew of him and my love for her poetry and her shewings has both nurtured and blinded me. God is as a memory. I reach out for Julian and find only her pictures. I reach out for God and find only an Icon that drew life from the love of a good woman.'

Again she stopped and waited, gazing always straight in front of her, intent on something that seemed to elude her, her brow contracted. 'But her death,' she murmured. 'Oh God, her death.' She wrote on, translating pictures into words, bright tears and wet ink:

'She lay on a straw pallet; the floor was grey and cold. A solitary late summer chrysanthemum straggled against the harsh light of the window. To be so close, so knowing; holding all, loving all, as the trees shed their leaves, shed and shed, you beholding all, loving all, embraced us, sweet, with the smell of dried roses. Embrace me yet again, while the trees lose their covering, oh my dear. I made a journey, a pilgrimage for your benediction, sweet saint. And now, loving all, each more inexpressibly tender, breath and sight and sound combine in one last chorus. I have made a further journey, following you always, a pilgrim for your benediction, sweet one, beholding less, but loving more though the trees are empty now and the leaves swept away. Croon you to sleep though, croon though I weep. Sleeping now, beholding us no more, and fading now, beholding not and on and on to the rising light. Numb we walk away and laugh a little.'

It was written and she would write of it no more. Picking up the torch she walked wearily back towards the warm centre of the house.

The snow fell heavily that winter. The fuchsia bush outside the house grew brown and frozen. When the snows melted only the brown dead twigs remained. As the sun grew stronger the dead growth yielded to fresh green shoots. She was glad. She wrote.

> I did not know the pain it cost
> To risk the heaving, earth cracked impulse
> Up.
> But I have seen the bending head
> And tender stem to pale against
> The heavy soil.

She lived alone that winter, trudging miles through the weary snow, allowing the icy winds to lash her cheeks and hair. Sometimes she screamed into the wind, cursing its indifference. At other times she allowed the great warm grief to flow till she was satisfied, or purged; she could not tell which.

That summer she left the house for a second time and set off west in the direction her friend had travelled many months before. She left before dawn, mounting the thin grey light and riding on through a passage of darkness until the sun warmed the yellowing summer fields. At evening she arrived in the village. The flies, companions of the day's irritations, left then while the sky promised heat for the following days. She rode in slowly and unobserved until she came to the stone church. Dismounting, she left her travelling companion and walked up the overgrown path to the left of the church where there stood a long, low house. Before she could knock a voice from behind called her softly; she turned and once more met the embrace of the sister she had left in the winter. The red of the sky gradually extinguished and went out as the two women, arm in arm, turned and went into the house.

It was now that the task of rebuilding began. They had often talked of what their shared life might be, but before there had always been Julian, the dreamer, whose shewings had sculpted them. Now they must ask for the prophetic gift for themselves. They seemed poised, but as they acted out their promises, her grief was always between them, spilling the wine and the bread. There was no faith in their eyes, and no comfort, just a challenge to build on rootlessness.

Sometimes she dreamed; a dream of logs drifting slowly and randomly towards the sea. She watched them jolt, turning slowly, indifferently, as they drifted by, lapped by the water their own motion made. Then the water was gone and the logs were bleaching in the wind and sunlight, drying, splintering, as if to anticipate the marks that the woodman's axe would make. She could hear the tearing wood as the axe fell. And so it must have been; embattled limbs on a dirty bed, not wanting nor desiring such a complex ending, the coupling of lust and indifference. Yet unasked and unasking she had come like a stranger into a room of preoccupied guests when none could point out the host. And now they were celebrating Advent, but longing for Christmas. So she thought of Mary and of the pain that concluded her advent and heralded the birth; and then the joy that conjured even angels in the empty skies – yet her son had been a stranger. Born from God's and Mary's womb, Christ was both stranger and host, the Banquet and the Priest. She tried to chase the image to its conclusion and see the Priest who broke his own body to feed the poor, but she had never been hungry, or poor, or naked. She looked at her arm and saw it was strong and capable.

But the paradox of a winter baby whose holy advent might redeem her own unholy birth stirred her. The flesh and the blood and the log and the axe she understood and was grateful for. Now she looked out over the bleached landscape to the point where the colourless sky met the icy ground. It called her to run and be baptised into death and resurrection in the white and silent snow. So she ran – past the thorn tree, past the hole in the stone where the water was held frozen within its swirling motion, and over the great rolling moor, eternally holding Julian's crumbling body. At the top of the moor she stood a second, then stretching out her arms wide, she threw herself cruciform into the snow.

Later that year the woman turned the pages of her book until she found a blank one. She wrote:

> Spring has planted roots for our branches and what we believed is come to pass. Love is all his meaning, though the roots grow slowly, forcing apart the years. The clay is unyielding and the rock hard, but the roots grow gently, breaking and welding. All that is seen comes to rest; securely, windblown and sometimes bent with grief, yet all that is seen and all that is unseen comes to rest.

Only Half the Story

Michelene Wandor

I wish I believed in God. When my mother died in June 1981 I wished I believed in God, because then I would have known where she'd gone. I could have talked to other people about where she'd gone, and I might have been able to anticipate going there too, and having all the conversations we had never had, and now would never have. Except of course that we would if we ended up in the same place. I hated the burial service and the rabbi rabbiting on about her being the Mother of Israel, and yet I was glad it was happening. I hated all the *facts*, the material, step-by-step, biological *facts* about death, all the things that are so cleverly and carefully concealed from us twentieth-century westerners. I did not want to know them. I still don't. But I did find the gathering together of unquestioning ritual a comforting event. The hours between the coffin coming into my parents' home and its disappearing under sticky Essex soil were valuable events. The men and women ranged on opposite sides of the cemetery chapel was offensive; the fact that we were all there was comforting. The walk to the grave was almost absurd, a ceremonial procession with no real purpose; the prayers at the grave were almost inaudible mumbles; the male relatives were instructed to throw some earth onto the coffin. I ignored the instruction and got my sister to join me in saying the only material goodbye we could say, to participate actively in recognising the fact that she had gone, to throw some earth in too. I took a stone out of my sister's hand, telling her she mustn't throw a stone in because my mother didn't like noise.

When we went back to the house I brought in a bottle of whisky that I had hidden in my car; my father had patriarchally (sic) said 'no alcohol'. I had ignored him (not the first time) and everyone sipped tiny tots of Famous Grouse out of their tea cups before they were refilled with tea. The immediate family were meant to sit on chairs down one side of the room – oh, the chairs. The story of the chairs. They are called *shiva* chairs. *Shiva* literally means 'seven' in Hebrew, and stands for the seven days of ritual mourning to be observed by the immediate family. During that time there is open house, friends and other relatives come to visit, to talk, to commiserate, and once a day the rabbi pops in to say prayers at home, with the family and whoever else is there. The immediate family is not meant to cook. They are meant to mourn, to be cared for by other relatives, friends and neighbours. The synagogue has special chairs, low chairs upon which the immediate family must sit during the *shiva*. On the morning of the funeral my brother and I had gone to collect such chairs from the local synagogue. They were rickety, uneven, full of tiny holes. I was furious. No way, I said, would my mother have let such rubbishy chairs into her plain, clean, houseproud house. I stayed outside while my brother took the two worst chairs in to show my father, and in five minutes' time, sure enough, he came back with the chairs, my father gesticulating in a rage, saying no way would these chairs come into his house. We took them back to the synagogue, the rabbi thanking us profusely for pointing out the woodworm, but us sitting on my father's own chairs did not go down at all well with him.

Well. Over the next seven days, people came to – pay their respects is the traditional phrase. I'm not so sure. It was a chance to have a quick look at distant relatives, at wealthy cousins bowed down, pale and looking twice their age with the burden of Stamford Hill Judaism. It was a chance to see family friends who had not seen me since I wore school uniform; it was something. Every evening the rabbi dropped in, the old men from the synagogue formed their minimum quorum of ten men (women, of course, do not count as people, therefore they cannot be counted, the Good Lord quite clearly wouldn't hear them however loudly they shouted). I even took some prickly, disenchanted comfort in the intoned ritual, the blessings, I even learned a little something. I learned that *goy*, the slang slightly contemptuous naming of a Christian, originally meant 'other people'. It was simply a way to distinguish 'them' from 'us', different from the more resounding word *Am* (pronounced with a long 'a') which means 'nation'. Death can teach you a thing or two.

Although we had our row of home-grown *shiva* chairs, I didn't always keep my place. I got up and made tea, or offered biscuits. One young religious family friend took my father aside and told him he shouldn't eat the soup I had cooked for him because it was unclean, since I was in mourning and shouldn't cook. She did, to do her credit, bring gefilte fish and salad for him. The rabbi knew I had children, and either guessed or was told that I was divorced. Everyone who comes to the funeral or later to the *shiva* is meant to shake hands with each member of the immediate family and wish them long life. The rabbi wished me long life at the funeral, but never again afterwards. His wife was friendly until she asked me what synagogue I belonged to, and I said 'none'. She didn't wish me long life either. She didn't even shake my hand. I desperately wanted to be wished long life in the face of death, by absolutely everyone in the whole world, even God would have been acceptable.

It's all over now. The practical, material, day-to-day worries have come back. There is a gap I don't understand. In words it looks like 'my mother died last summer', in feelings and meanings it means something I do not begin to understand. Well, perhaps I am beginning to understand, because I am writing this. It is the first time I have really had to deal with death, and if the ritual had not been there I would have found it a hundred times harder. The ritual meant that over a period of days there was a constant reminder that the living had to come to terms with death. The ritual could only supply a kind of sending-off party, a collective nod to the end of life, before turning back to the business of getting on with living. I was and am grateful for the ritual. I hate the institutions it derives from, I scoff at the abstraction of the beliefs it has to entail. There is clearly no such thing as God. (Please don't send a thunderbolt until you have heard me out.) If I had lived a century ago I would have been a Darwinist; science holds the answers to the evolution of the world, to the cycles of natural life, socialism holds the answers to the way life should be organised in the future, feminism holds the answers to the place of women in that future life. But biological decay alone does not explain the meaning of death, the Buddhist belief of the eternal renewal cycle isn't enough; reincarnation is an attractive idea. It will give my mother another chance. She could be the person I would have liked her to be, or she can have another go entirely at doing her own thing. I could get to believe in reincarnation more easily than I could get to believe in God, because it makes every encounter a new excitement, a new possibility. Is this her? What will she come back as?

My children and I joke sporadically; she is in heaven with Buddy Holly, Elvis and Janis Joplin, cooking them chicken soup. If anyone needs it, they do. She is busy looking after the Messiah, so that when he (of course it's a he) decides to come down he will have all his clean clothes ready. A woman's work is never done. Anyone who dies will be welcomed by my mother's shortbread biscuits, made only with butter. Heaven in this scenario is teeming with hip folk; it is a carefully screened cultural mecca. No pious angels, but a world in our own desired image, in which we have created our own Mother of Israel. On reflection, I'm not sure I would be better off believing in God. But when my mother died, I found that I was glad that some people still do.

Until the Real Thing Comes Along

Anna Briggs

I suppose this all started when I read an issue of *Red Rag*, one of the feminist journals, in the late seventies. The cover indicated straight away that the writers were taking a swipe at romance, and all that went under the name of 'lerv'. Inside, one writer denounced love as a reactionary force, keeping women down; another defined something I had never heard of before – couplism – and in the same breath condemned it. From what I remember, couplism was a social form where people in affectionate couples (hetero- or homo-sexual) effectively excluded 'single' people from their lives and from many forms of social activity.

I read this at a time when I was a closet Christian in the women's movement, and vice versa. Though I felt deeply uneasy and unhappy at the conclusions formed by these writers – that love was suspect, that people should not form close affectionate relationships – I could not fault their arguments. It was true – love, *as we knew it*, was keeping women in their place. Loving and supporting men, as husbands/lovers, sons, workmates, comrades, was something we did not know how to give up, though we found it endlessly frustrating and often unreciprocated. At a time when it wasn't 'done' in the movement to admit to having a close relationship with a man, it seemed impossible to get women to discuss what they really felt – and did – about these relationships.

Then a year or so after reading that *Red Rag*, I heard Una Kroll speak, powerfully and poignantly, on the theme 'I come to bring not peace, but a sword'. This is a teaching of Jesus which gives many Christians a lot of trouble; the notion of dividing 'father from son and mother from daughter' seems uncannily close to the activities of political youth movements of the extreme right or left. Una's interpretation of this seemed to me inspired and wise, especially coming from a woman who has been pilloried by many churchmen for her boat-rocking activities in the cause of women's ordination. She talked about a church which was frightened of using conflict constructively. She claimed that it *was* loving to confront people when you believed them to be wrong, especially if their actions were hurting or oppressing you. It *was not* loving to allow people to carry on hurting you. It *was* loving to demand that they behave like human beings.

While these ideas were rolling around in my mind I was constantly aware of being close to, and part of, a daily experience: women agonised in their minds and with each other for hours about the relationships they had, how much they poured into them, how little effect it seemed to have. Women used each other's love and support to bind up their broken spirits during the day, ready for a fresh mental, if not physical, assault at night. Some had men whose tempers were often out of control, and who demolished their women with brickbats of sarcasm and innuendo day after day. Others had landed the 'strong silent' types whose method was just to ignore differences, to refuse to discuss them, to lapse into silence for hours on end. Marriages were breaking up, as my own had earlier, when women got to the end of their tether and pulled out. Again and again I saw relationships end when the woman gave up. Then the old familiar pattern appeared: a woman unable to care any more about a man, who's going down on his knees, showering her with gifts, taking the kids out for a good time – all the things he didn't do when they were together. I found that it wasn't in the women's movement, but where 'two or three women were gathered together' that the deepest discussions about the problem of love in heterosexual relationships occurred. Most of these discussions did not include any hopes of change – indeed my views of men were rosy compared to some of my sisters' who hoped for and got little or nothing from their men. Fundamentally women felt that they were expected to work on the principle that if you kept on pouring love into someone – building him up, confirming him, not criticising him, not answering back, not complaining when he hurt you – it would all come right in the end – HE would realise how valuable your love was and return it. But it just wasn't happening like that. For too many women the exercise was more like pouring water into sand. It distressed me even more when women resorted to living 'in their own head', cutting off from their man emotionally as the only way to stay sane; or when they talked about 'managing him' and 'getting round him'. I was fairly sure this wasn't love either.

What was to be done? I knew that, however much the *Red Rag* writers, and other feminists including me might want it, women for a variety of reasons would not give up living with men. So I wanted to offer some of the insights of the Christian faith to feminism and vice versa. I hoped we could find out what this bogus love we had been sold really was, and what real love should be. I also wanted to find out if other Christians believed in the distorted version of love taught by the church over the ages, which has been a great source of oppression to women.

Why did I think love was important at all? I am now at the stage where I would define my Christianity thus: I don't know what people mean by 'god' except that it/she/he is another name for love, which I recognise as a positive and creative force in the world, and without which we might as well (and probably soon will) be dead. I recognise the existence of Jesus whose complex and perplexing teachings, related imperfectly by puzzled hearers, ring bells for me about the meaning of our own lives and the 'human condition'. Love is supremely important to me as the driving force of the world because of the way it keeps seeping and bursting through when we think all is bleak and hopeless. I only recognise love, or 'god' if you want to use that word, through other people.

Just about the time I was trying to tie up these ideas, I picked up *Love's Endeavour, Love's Expense* by W.H. Vanstone,[1] and found that some of his definitions of what Christians (should) mean by love were rather helpful. I was interested in his contention that the characteristics of fatherly love – god as stern Victorian father, impervious to our failings – were a distortion of the real meaning of the love of god, and the god of love; this view of god only served to drive people away. Vanstone was saying that we could not love a god whom we had to fear and who could not be hurt by us. We could not have a loving relationship with anybody who bestowed love as a favour, and who did not need our love in return. I don't know how Vanstone's theme struck male readers, but I certainly found in it echoes of my own problems with the father god, with whom I could not identify at all. That the church has managed to create this image of god in the face of the vulnerability of Jesus in the Gospels is testimony to something – and from my point of view it looks suspiciously like the male orientation of the church itself.

So I started off with some of the Vanstone's definitions of love, added some of my own, and tried to fit them in or round some feminist insights. These are Vanstone's main points:

– Love is not control. Anyone who seeks to control another person is not showing love.

– Love is vulnerable, characterised by self-giving. Loving in any form leaves the person who loves open to rejection, hurt and pain. If it was impervious to hurt, it would not be love as Jesus taught it.

– Love needs recognition. Loving actions aren't done for

recognition, in fact they must be done selflessly – but to flourish they need recognition. A paradox here: by the very nature of its selflessness, love demands recognition though it doesn't ask for it.

I've added some thoughts of my own which develop those ideas:

– Love must be given freely. It should not be expected as a duty, an obligation, something owed – this is not to say that people do not have a responsibility for the well-being of these they have shown love to, but that overall the way they show this love must be authentic. Though you can sometimes do something out of a sense of obligation, if an action is always carried out for this reason, or because of fear, eventually love goes out of it. Then, even if the form is the same, the action becomes empty of meaning.

– Love does not avoid conflict. It is a distortion of love to hide true feelings, to use manipulation and cunning instead of directness even when this causes conflict.

– In a loving relationship, one person cannot be sure they know what's best for the other – or seek to impose it (this is a development of Vanstone's first point). Guidance and direction offered in a loving relationship need to be related to the actual emotional and social maturity of the loved person, not to fantasies and stereotypes.

– To love anybody else you must love yourself. This has often been denied by church teaching, but experience in so many fields has shown that people who hate themselves, and regard themselves as unlovable, inadequate, useless, rarely have the strength to make loving relationships. Often they only get the chance to discover that they are lovable, and can love in return, if they are surrounded by a particular sort of loving concern coming from other people. This creative loving does not have to be endlessly tolerant and can involve using conflict creatively, make demands and stand up to unreasonableness; but its aim is to drown self-fear and self-hatred in the overall security of the relationship.

I don't feel very optimistic when I compare what I've observed about male/female relationships with this set of guidelines. It seems to me that women have learned that we are intrinsically worthless, mainly to be valued for the ability to produce other lives. To fulfil *our* lives we must act through another person. We acquire status and respect by getting, and keeping, a good husband. The way many widows find themselves cut off from social contact even with former 'friends' shows how completely vicarious this existence is. A spinster is an object of pity, an incomplete person, a failure. In contrast, men are taught to see themselves as complete individuals, with a high sense of self-regard; the bachelor is a complete person, even someone to be envied. Though other factors, like race and class, affect people's self-perception, within each group men, not women, are the real people (phrases like 'trade unionists and their wives' make this all too clear). What men do or think matters in the world. Education, and particularly public school 'education for leadership', gradually weans men away from women – mothers, sisters, grannies, etc. – so that they are brought up to see us as unnecessary to their fulfilment. Men who go to prep school, public school and then on to all-male establishments like army academies and, until recently, theological colleges, may learn vaguely that they will 'need a wife', but they may never learn to *love* women.

Women learn that the creation and maintenance of love is our province and our duty. Our love is not to be given freely, but as part of the 'contract' of a relationship. Many explanations have been given for this – ranging from folk-belief to social science. Start with, 'Man's love is of his life a thing apart, 'tis women's whole existence', and end at the 'instrumental-expressive' polarity of human capabilities devised by Talcott Parsons (which essentially says that men are good with things, women are good with people); examine all points in between – including the highly convenient pseudo-Freudian idea (trotted out by agony aunties every time a woman complains of finding porn mags in the wardrobe) that woman's whole being is involved in her sexual activity, while for men it is a biological urge from which their highest thoughts are detached (shades of the early church fathers) and you can see the scale of the problem. If men and women believe, or act as though they believed, that love and loving actions are 'natural' for women and not for men, they will not be able to fulfil the criteria of love that I've outlined. If love is natural for women it cannot be given freely; it is expected, only the absence of it will cause comment. This is what women mean when they say they are taken for granted. Once actions, which started as a part of loving, are taken for granted, their loving origins become distorted and they are done with resentment: the givers often despise and resent the people whom they serve for not seeing the love behind the actions, for not reciprocating.

It's here that the test of recognition comes in. As Vanstone puts it, loving actions are not done for recognition, but demand it. Through a power structure and culture which sees women's selflessness as a natural characteristic, it is possible to avoid recognising our actions as a conscious expression of love. There are so many manifestations of this: from moving to a strange town because of a husband's job, to giving up paid work to look after elderly relatives. So many of the things that women do out of love are treated as natural biological developments and are not thought worthy of comment. Many people whom I've spoken to in organisations for disabled people have asserted that marriages break up much more often because of the disability of the wife than of the husband – apparently women are more likely to see the care of a disabled husband as an extension of their loving service, while men are more likely to view the prospect of altering their lives radically in the selfless service of a disabled wife as just too much to bear. To put it another way – a husband just has to *be* but there are certain things a woman must *do* to be a proper wife.

Women have also learned that one of our duties in the maintenance of love is the avoidance of conflict – which is why yielding is also portrayed as a natural characteristic in women, but a weakness in men. What women are supposed to learn instead is how to manage and manipulate men – so cunning is another supposed female trait. There is no denying that women have become past-mistresses in this art, but that must be seen in the context of our lack of access of direct power and openness. It is often easier to be cunning and to gain limited objectives than to be open and cause conflict, but cunning in relationships is no part of love. Pretending, cunning and manipulation distort their practitioner and lead to a breakdown in communication, a lessening of loving vulnerability on both sides. It is an essential of cunning that it successfully fools the object, who is then despised for being so easily fooled. The fact that this has been praised as an attribute of women throughout Christendom doesn't say much for the integrity of Christian culture. Describing this way of operating in a relationship as 'loving' also means that love is being equated with control, albeit control by devious and underhand means.

If women continue to use manipulation instead of being open, to pretend, as so many women have done, that what hurts isn't painful, then men will never understand what behaviour and attitudes do hurt, do fail to come up to our expectations of love. The theme of love and conflict is one that bears a lot more examination and discussion. How do you use conflict constructively in a close relationship? How can someone who feels powerless take the risk of causing conflict to clear the lines of communication about her powerlessness? How can we stop those old labels being used whenever we try to air something ('you're always nagging')? Why do so many men seem to feel so threatened by the idea of airing conflict?

One of the issues that enters the ring here is the idea of forgiveness. We have been given to understand that forgiveness is very powerful, and in fact an obligatory virtue. The idea, first expounded by Paul, that love 'beareth all things, believeth all things, hopeth all things, endureth all things' has entered the consciousness of many people in a Christian and even post-Christian culture – being able to forgive is obviously part of this. I think this has been responsible for a lot of the guilt that accompanies any failure to forgive, any unwillingness to keep on bearing impossible behaviour by women. This has reproached the battered woman when she eventually leaves; it has reproached any woman who pulls out, mentally or physically, because she has had enough. But the trouble with forgiveness is that its healing power is lost if the person you are forgiving thinks either that he hasn't done anything that needs forgiveness, or that if he has it was *your* fault anyway. If you're just making a fuss about nothing, or you're a jealous bitch, or a nagging old shrew, you can't be forgiving. Blaming women has become one of the central pillars of the way the system works. It's *our* fault if our son or husband turns into a mass murderer or rapist; if he drinks, beats us, stays out all night or turns to another woman for comfort. All over the place, women are asking themselves in their heads, 'What have *I* done wrong?' There is no chance of forgiveness and healing if the man has done nothing he should be sorry for. I remember a midwife telling me recently that over half the women who give birth say, 'I'm sorry' (about their 'conduct' in labour), as soon as it is over. With women being sorry for more than we are responsible for, and men for far less, there is no chance for forgiveness to be part of growth in male/female relationships.

The image of love which has been given to men is one that involves control, *in*vulnerability, the right to dictate the self-image and life of their 'beloved'. They aren't encouraged to build a partner up and affirm her value as part of love. We see this one-way traffic in emotional support in every human activity – and throughout political parties, churches and other organisations, men's reaction to women withdrawing our support is out of all proportion to the often very limited demands that women are making. Or is it a sign that men really do understand the wider implicit demands that women are making, for a return of support, a reciprocation of love, an equal share with the 'housework' of the world, and an opening up, a discovering of their own vulnerability?

The use of sexuality has got mixed up, almost inextricably, with both 'love as control' and 'love as manipulation', so that it is almost impossible to dissociate sexuality from these cultural, political and social implications. The conditions of women's lives, once they form a loving heterosexual attachment, have been stringently defined. That is why I found a statement in the *Lichfield Report*, the Church of England's latest report on marriage, so amazing: the writers claimed that there are 'few if any external constraints on marriage'. I don't know if the members of the commission which wrote this were familiar with the social security or tax laws, but they surely can't have failed to notice that churches (in as much as they act as surrogates for state registrars) are mixed up in a very nasty piece of inverse legislation concerning marriage: A woman cannot charge her husband (unless legally separated) with rape. Now the meaning of this is clearly that a husband has a right to sexual intercourse at any time, whatever the woman feels about it. So whatever the prayers at the marriage service may say, the sexual love of a woman is not freely given on each occasion when we wish to give it, as it is the right of the husband anyway. This makes nonsense of any notion of loving freely and expressing it sexually. That the church has got mixed up with this state of affairs is 'an offence and a scandal'. Similarly, refusal by wives to have intercourse has been a matrimonial cause for men (but not vice versa). The churches have also been involved in perpetuating the power of legitimacy which has been a most powerful 'external constraint' on women's social and sexual behaviour, while for men having children 'on the wrong side of the blanket' has been seen as a sign of virility or at worst as a peccadillo. 'Giving your children a name' has been such a pre-occupation for women that we have given birth in secret (and lost babies through lack of perinatal assistance), been sent away in disgrace, murdered, disinherited, disowned and pressured into adoption or more recently abortion. Logically, the safest name to give a child is its mother's, but legitimacy (and recent government proposals to extend paternal rights to children born out of wedlock show this is still so) is the foundation stone of men's control of our reproductive capacity. Having all this mixed up with supposedly loving relationships makes it very difficult to believe in the integrity of that love.

The women's movement's concern with regaining 'control' is a valid response to this state of affairs. We have learned from men that the desirable state to be in is one of 'control', so we demand the right to control our bodies, fertility, sexual activity, etc. A recent feature in *Spare Rib* (no. 104) gave a revealing picture of women currently trying to regain control over their sexuality. The trouble with this is that control is being confused with having an equal ability to say what ensues when two people have close physical contact. All sorts of unexpected things happen when people try to control things – and sex between two people who are both trying to control it strikes me as a very cold sort of bargaining situation. Are we trying to gain control, or to get men to stop controlling us? Unless you're contending that sexual activity should have little to do with love, I can't see control as a worth-while objective in sexual activity. The same applies to controlling our bodies as so much that happens to our bodies is to do with our relationships. We can demand the right to control our fertility, but watch the efforts of women to regain it when they've got to thirty-five and it's on the wane or damaged by the birth control they've been using. We can demand the right to self-definition and mobility, but end up in a wheelchair because of an accident or a progressive disease. To live in a loving world, we should be trying to get men to adopt our 'traditional' openness and vulnerability, not trying to control our relationships with people, and with the world about us (look where *that's* got us). One of the insights which Christianity can offer liberation movements is surely that life and living are gifts, to be used sensitively, and that love and openness can be the most powerful forces in life. Living a loving life is costly and makes us vulnerable; and one thing that the women's movement has to do is make the costliness visible – end the old myth that love is part of our biological make-up, not something learned (at great expense) from our mothers and foremothers. There's no reason to throw love away, but we have to refine it and show up the cheap imitations.

This has been most painful to write, but I've felt impelled to do it because I really believe that ignoring love leads to death and we may as well not be here if we live by any other principle. I can't say that I end up on an optimistic note about love and its success in overcoming greed, selfishness, laziness, etc. Some days I think, it's going to come through, it's worth being true to what I've come to believe about real love. Other days I'm completely depressed and think it's all a waste of time: why don't I just follow all the other women who lie and deceive, pander to men and live from day to day and year to year without sorting out the major issues between themselves and their men, because it's less trouble and less risky? I get *most* depressed when I'm told, 'I love you,' after a big unresolved quarrel. Depressed, because the statement is a substitute for sorting things out and is no consolation to me at all. To such a statement, one of my sisters replied: 'Well, if that's the case, I'm just grateful you don't hate me.'

But I am fairly clear now that I would have to cut loose or break out of an inauthentic situation because of what I believe. I do understand that causes and liberation movements are empty and joyless without love. It is where there is love that they sparkle the most, not where they're dedicated to wresting 'control' from oppressors. It's the love and music in the Latin American liberation movements which is the most moving, and which gives me cause to believe that they will be successful in the end. It's the genuine rejoicing at yet another woman's discovery of her own worth and love-li-ness which is one of the most positive things in the women's movement. If we can teach that to our daughters and bring our sons up in this love (teach them that being feminised is not the same as being emasculated), we'll be getting somewhere. The church needs to redefine its god of love, to get rid of the monopoly of father imagery ('Motherlike she tends and spares us'!) and stop perpetuating the distortion of what we are dimly trying to understand as love. We need to stop hearing from the pulpit about the strength of Jesus and the receptive selflessness of Mary and other such false divisions – they were *both* strong and *both* receptive. We women need to learn to love ourselves, to be open, honest, to shun manipulation and cunning, to stop concealing pain. Men need to learn to lose control, to leave the centre of the stage sometimes, to be vulnerable, to stop defining us, to recognise love instead of taking it for granted and to take equal responsibility for creating and nurturing love. Then we can all grow up together.

Everything the Pope Ever Wanted to Know about Sex and Didn't Dare to Ask

Maggie Redding

I thought it was difficult enough being a Christian and a feminist until I began announcing myself as Catholic and lesbian. Sometimes I feel I don't exist. As a woman I am wiped out anyway by the male language and power structures of the church. Any discussion in the Catholic Church of women's situation is limited usually to topics like 'women's role' – we are an afterthought, an extra and as such a problem. 'Men's role' is never questioned, it is assumed, taken for granted.

But as women we are expected to be wives and mothers, roles that are seen as having a very lowly status and no individual identity. The only women to achieve any recognition in the Catholic Church are nuns (sexless women) – and even nuns still usually find themselves playing the same subordinate role to bishops and clergy as wives do to husbands. Too often they are still channelled into the 'low status' work – with children, the elderly, the sick. The work may be essential in any society, but in ours it is not recognised as valuable.

Lesbian women are then subjected to additional diminishment. Women are not expected to be sexual persons and so to define oneself publicly by one's sexual orientation is seen as a particular threat. We are also subsumed into the negative category of male homosexuality, which is strongly condemned and badly misunderstood by the Catholic Church. And finally, as women without a man through whom to live, we are totally unseen and unheard.

The Catholic Church, more than other Christian denominations, finds all questions of sexuality an embarrassment. On the one hand, there is the church's very fine contemporary teaching on social justice and concern for the poor and oppressed; on the other, there is the authoritarian tradition of Catholicism with its right to make pronouncements and declarations on all sorts of subjects and its underdeveloped, antiquated theology of sexuality. These two strands meet and find themselves in conflict when it comes to questions relating to both women and homosexuality. For instance the church's official teaching includes:

> All forms of social and cultural discrimination . . . on
> the grounds of sex, race, colour, social conditions,
> language or religion, must be curbed and eradicated as
> incompatible with God's design. It is regrettable that
> these basic personal rights are not yet being respected
> everywhere, as is the case with women who are denied
> the chance freely to choose a husband, or a state of life,
> or to have access to the same educational and cultural
> benefits as are available to men.[1]

But women are still officially forbidden to serve at the altar, let alone given 'the chance freely to choose a state of life', be it priesthood or lesbianism. These conflicting strands create a real dilemma for the Catholic Church. Lesbian women who are Catholics are the epitomy of the dilemma.

Being Catholic and lesbian I present a problem to other Catholics who take their Christianity seriously. They have to love me; they cannot reject me, but neither can they condone me nor accept me. I, and the few other Catholic lesbian women who have not stormed out of the church in disgust, are walking reminders of the crisis of Catholicism. By not leaving the church, despite what the church does to us, we lay claim to the definition of the church as the People of God. We are the church.

It sounds a confident claim, but behind lies the pain and frustration of being at the receiving end of fear and caution whenever I ask Catholics for help and receive rejection. I have a problem: I feel I have to forgive the church for the way that it has treated me as a lesbian woman, but I cannot, yet.

The church's position on homosexuality and its position on women are related. To become a father, to procreate, to dominate, was the ideal and the need of the Old Testament Hebrew male. This procreative attitude to sex has been handed down into Christianity and, particularly, still forms the explicit base of Roman Catholic sexual ethics. It is reinforced by the 'awful warnings' in the stories of, for example, Onan – condemned to death for wasting semen – and Sodom and Gomorrah. The practice of male homosexuality was so abhorrent (partly because of its pagan cultic associations, partly because it involved a man acting like a woman, and partly because it was non-procreative) that laws and taboos against it have proliferated down the centuries. The church has treated these laws and the assumptions made in myths (that homosexuality could be equated with decadence and associated with pagans, and that it threatened tribal solidarity, for example) literally and ahistorically as true *facts*. Unfortunately, women who also relate to members of their own sex have had these and other assumptions and myths about homosexuality forced onto them, whether or not they actually relate to us. We are denied male privileges, but share male guilt.

In 1975, the Sacred Congregation for the Doctrine of the Faith issued a document called 'A Declaration on Certain Questions Concerning Sexual Ethics'.[2] In it we are told: 'homosexuals must certainly be treated with understanding and sustained in the hope of overcoming their personal difficulties and their inability to fit into society.' Any steps that the Catholic Church takes towards understanding homosexuality are steps towards understanding male homosexuality; therefore the assumption that all homosexuals are male is allowed to stand. The very existence of lesbianism is ignored in this document.

Moreover the very idea of 'understanding' as expressed here is offensive. I do not want to be 'understood'. I do not want well-meaning heterosexuals probing into my mind because *they* need to understand me. And 'homosexuals must be sustained in the hope of overcoming their personal difficulties'. I do not have personal difficulties because I am a lesbian. I have social difficulties. It is now seven years since that declaration was promulgated: and still no Catholic has come forward, as such, to 'sustain in her difficulties' a lesbian mother fighting for the custody of her children. I do not have an 'inability to fit into society'; society, and particularly the church, is the party that is suffering this inability.

The Vatican declaration says – generously? meaninglessly? – that the 'state of homosexuality' itself is morally neutral, but its practice is disordered and wrong. Because, as my copy of the New Catechism helpfully explains: 'Ultimately all homosexual (or rather homoerotic) tendencies come up against the discovery that the sexual in man can only find its natural fulfilment – as may be deduced from human structure – in the other sex.'[3]

I have to ask myself, what celibate Roman Catholic priest has ever looked at women's structure, or even attempted to understand its functions? If they had they might realise that the structures of sexual pleasure and of procreation are, in women, separate, and very often do not function simultaneously. In women at least non-procreative sexual pleasure is not a perversion but a difference.

But the adulation of procreativity, which has adversely affected male homosexuality, affects all women too. The situation concerning women's sexuality today is very similar to the time in the

fourth century when it was finally decided, after much delibera-
tion and by one vote at a church council, that women have souls.
At the present time, it seems there is a faint dawning in some
circles, though probably not ecclesiastical, that women have positive sexual experiences. I await the ninety-ninth Vatican Council
sometime in the twenty-fifth century when it will be decided,
by one vote of course, that yes, theologically women do have
orgasms – i.e., that women can have autonomous, positive, non-
procreative sexual experience. That will be a beginning of the
change in the church's teaching on all aspects of sexuality.

I often think that the procreation/sex problem is a bit like poor
old Galileo's problem in the fifteenth century when he was made
to recant his statement that the earth revolved around the sun. His
factual observation was denied because it did not fit into the
church's theory. I gather they have reinstated him fairly recently –
only four hundred years later. Is it possible that in AD 2382 some
pope will reinstate women and sex by saying that yes, procreation
does revolve around sexuality and not, as had been firmly believed,
that sexuality revolved around procreation? After all, the total
silence on women's sexuality, the awful embarrassment that
lesbian women cause, the oppression we suffer is the same as
making us recant.

Obviously the historical and social, not to mention religious,
reasons for the suppression of women's sexuality are many and
complex. I had a new insight recently. In the June 1980 edition of
the *New Internationalist*, I read:

> Millions of people in the developing world want large
> families. Where there are no old-age pensions, no
> medical services and no unemployment pay, children
> are the main source of economic security. Where the
> task of fetching wood and water and tending animals
> takes up to twelve hours a day, children are an asset in

the family's struggle for survival. Where infant
mortality rates are high, many children are necessary to
ensure the survival of some.[4]

What struck me was that the article was describing the sort of
society that received and evolved the Mosaic law. What time or
energy or motive had they to give, not just to questions of homosexuality or women's erotic response, but to sexuality at all? Did
they have sex for pleasure or merely to survive? I even wondered if
male sexuality, either as we know it now, or as it might develop
devoid of male power, was suppressed too? Was sex a desperate
activity to keep the race going, a duty almost? Were children in
such a simple society accumulated like capital is in western society
today? (Why does the Pope condemn contraception now?)

But wait, I thought, there is another aspect to this. What
happens when, for one reason or another, these simple societies
become stable and don't need to expand? What happens to the
surplus sexual activity? Could this account for the relatively more
relaxed attitudes to homosexuality, the growing awareness in
women of their own sexuality, for the fact these are now issues? Is
this our dilemma – surplus sexuality?

The people of the Old Testament, who never reached this point
in their development, needed to create population growth and
stability. They introduced various laws concerning sexual activity,
along with others about things like property and ritual, to help
create stability, internal peace and group identity. But these
laws are not 'natural' or immutable. What about other simple
societies? Why is polyandry accepted? Not necessarily because
women are particularly aware of their own sexual needs. Could it
be because it is a way of controlling births? One woman with four
husbands can have only one baby a year, fewer if she is breast-
feeding. In another society, four heterosexual couples could
generate four babies a year. In yet another society, four men with

four wives each could produce sixteen babies in a year.

What I am getting at is that there are ways of organising sexuality according to the economic or other needs of a given society. Even the expression of sexuality can be so organised. Among the Etoro, heterosexual intercourse is taboo for between 205 and 260 days a year. What do they do during all that time? Perhaps Pope Paul VI only told us half the truth when he issued *Humanae Vitae* condemning contraception. I suspect the Etoro along with other societies can happily accept that there are more ways of expressing sexuality and enjoying sexual experience than copulation.

As Gayle Rubin writes in *Towards an Anthropology of Women*: 'The realm of human sex, gender and procreation has been subjected to and changed by relentless social activity for millenia. Sex as we know it – gender, identity, sexual desire and fantasy, concepts of childhood – is itself a social product.'[5]

When the Catholic Church speaks of 'natural fulfilment' it is ignoring the known facts to fit its own theories.

Because of the ignorance about the clitoris and female biology generally and the silence of women on their authentic sexual experiences, men have been able to impose a notion of sexuality that is entirely in male interests, not just in relationship to women, but within the whole family and wider society. It strikes me as shocking that all the declarations and opinions handed out by the Catholic Church are founded on wilful ignorance. For instance the church's teachings on sexual anthropology are still using Thomistic theology – and Thomas Aquinas believed that biologically women contributed nothing at all except a nurturing place to the life of a new child which was created fully complete in the man's sperm. If sex between men and women was not understood as consisting only of copulation-for-procreation, what problems would be solved? *There* is the church's answer to the vexed questions of contraception, abortion, sterilisation. But because of women's powerlessness in the church and because of the way lesbian women are wiped out of mental existence, the answers to these questions which we Catholic lesbian women could offer the church remain unvoiced.

The church continues to condemn any sexual act which does not lead to procreation – with the exception of infertile couples, those past the age of procreation and 'safe period' sex, of course. (And even these exceptions ought to raise doubts about the whole teaching.) Yet, at the same time, we are taught that we must follow our consciences, and that our consciences must be fully informed and developed. Frankly my conscience is more informed than those of the celibate men who make such rules. I *know* how my body, a female body, functions. More people should know that genital stimulation without penetration can lead to greater pleasure for women, less anxiety about pregnancy, contraception, abortion and so on, and potentially to greater flexibility and equality in a relationship.

Homosexuality and women's sexuality pose similar problems for a church which wants to cling to procreative sex as the only 'natural' or 'good' sexual expression. Identical lines of thought can be seen in *Humanae Vitae* and in the 'Declaration on Certain Questions of Sexual Ethics'. In *Humanae Vitae* (which means 'On Human Life') male sexuality, as expressed in the West in present times, *is* sexuality. Indeed, one of the arguments against contraception is that 'it may lead a husband to make excessive and inconsiderate demands on his wife'.[6] Good positive thinking in one way – almost a condemnation of rape in marriage. It does not seem to have occurred to the authors that a woman could make excessive and inconsiderate demands on her husband, nor that a string of pregnancies could be excessive and inconsiderate and much more too.

Similarly the 1975 Vatican 'Declaration' says that: 'According to the objective moral order, homosexual relations are acts which lack an essential and indispensible finality.'

Objective? I feel privileged to be able to see, because I am a woman and because I am a lesbian, that this way of looking at the moral order is not objective at all. It is in the interests of men. Essential to whom? Indispensible to whom?

Indeed, as 'there can be no contradiction between two divine laws – that which governs the transmitting of life and that which governs the fostering of married love', let us separate them and reveal the vested interests for what they are.

To me, it is a source of frustration and anger that the Catholic Church's social teaching, so radical and so positive, is virtually unknown within and outside the church; yet the area of sexuality, where the teaching is so undeveloped and oppressive, is known to everyone in and out of the church.

The same church that produced the 'Declaration' of 1975 and *Humanae Vitae* in 1968, can also produce the following:

> Considerations of justice and equity can at times demand that those in power pay more attention to the weaker members of society seeing these are at a disadvantage when it comes to defending their own rights, asserting their legitimate interests.[7]

> More than any other, the individual who is animated by true charity labours skilfully to discover the causes of misery, to find the means to combat it, to overcome it resolutely. A creator of peace, he/she will follow her/his path, lighting the lamps of joy and playing their brilliance and loveliness on the hearts of men and women across the surface of the globe, leading them to recognise across all frontiers the faces of their sisters and brothers, the faces of their friends.[8]

In fact, it is this acute awareness of questions of justice that keeps me in the Catholic Church and gives me hope. The injustices against me as a lesbian help me to understand and identify with those who also experience injustice for various reasons. Through accepting my sexual orientation in the face of rejection by family, church and society, I have come to value myself as a person and am learning to recognise the personhood of others. I know that to offer help, tolerance, sympathy is to take away a person's dignity because when I am offered help because I am a woman, or sympathy because I am lesbian, I feel my personal dignity is affronted. I know that what I want is justice and I am learning to recognise that need in others. I cannot desert the church because there are people there, women too, and lesbian women. I cannot reject something that has made me what I am – my faith – anymore than I can reject my sexuality because that too is a part of who I am. To those who say that the Catholic Church is the archetypal patriarchal institution, I reply that it is not the institution that attracts me, but the church as movement. I would say also that every other institution in our society could be described as patriarchal also, and we cannot opt out of living unless we die. Catholic lesbian women have a prophetic role to play in the church – prophesy being more than seeing into the future, it is reading the signs of the times. We are a sign of the times in which we live by our very existence – we have something to say about sexuality, about justice, about faith and about forgiveness. Whether the church is seen as the Bride of Christ, Mother Church, the Scarlet Woman of Rome or a Dying Institution, she loves me, like a mother, unconditionally. And sometimes, like a mother, not understanding. And I can't help loving her. The church is the people, the church is us too – Catholic lesbian women.

Talking with God in the Green Fertile Valley
or
A Kind of Madness

Audrey Dunn

So here we are God, in Eden again.
I am naked before you.
No angels between us.
Just you and me.
Just like it was then.

It's going to be difficult,
I mean, I am recording our conversation.
Some of them will not like it back there
And not many of them will believe it.

Have you anything to say to that?

                    No.

Well that's great.
It's so convenient
For you to be silent.

Oh God!

                    I love you.

Love, love,
Oh don't talk to me
About love.
It's such a useless word.

> Well, I'm sorry
> But it's the best one we could think of
> Up here
> It seemed appropriate
> For you English.

> There are others
> Agape, philos, eros. . .

Eros, yes,
I'd rather not think about that one
Just now.
I've got this problem.

> I know you've got this problem.

I know you know I've got this problem.

I'll tell you something
It's no problem up here.

What do you mean?
And please
Take that smile off your face.

So you're not going to answer.
It's too easy for you gods.
Are you playing some kind of game with me?

Yes.

Yes?

I believe you.

I hope you know what you're doing.
I don't want this to be
The end of our relationship.
I can't do without you you see.
You know that do you?
I hope you know that.

The water beneath this bridge
Is powerful.
I could hear it in the night.
Its power draws me.

The power within me
Is too much for me.

Where does all this water rush to,
A weir, a black hole?
Are you afraid of the black hole?
Are you afraid of your own power?

But you are silent.
What do you say God?
What do you say?

I
My child
Say
'Wait and see,'
Like your mother
Used to say.

Hm! You are a God of few words,
But go on,
You can have the last one.

Thanks.

Women in the Peace Movement

Fiona Cooper

There have always been women working for peace, holding bazaars, making tea after meetings, and generally being supportive; but today an enormous and growing number of women are taking the initiative in peace work. Greenham Common Women's Peace Camp, started in September 1981 to oppose the installation of cruise missiles, has inspired camps outside military bases and nuclear installations in Scotland, all over Europe, and recently in the USA. There is a proliferation of women's peace organisations: the Women's Peace Alliance, Women Oppose the Nuclear Threat, Mothers for Peace, The Women's International League for Peace and Freedom, Women for Life on Earth, The Women's Pentagon Action – the list is much longer and growing daily.

There are many reasons for this recent growth in activity. One of the main ones is the government's plan to site cruise missiles at Greenham Common in December 1983. This decision was taken without reference to the people of this country, although it involves first-strike weapons: their presence here would make us a target in the event of nuclear war. Despite this, our government would not have any control over when or why they were used. The idea of a 'limited' nuclear war is being shown up as nonsensical. Scientists are arguing not over how many people would die, but over how many 'megadeaths' each person would suffer. The deadly dispute continues while the (literal) deadline draws nearer.

This is just one of the many things that has made ordinary women get up and act – to defend their lives and the lives of those they love and care for. Women who go and live in the peace camps say that they are leaving home for peace, just as for centuries men have left home for war. Men have been conditioned to reject peacefulness as unmasculine, too passive, something to be encouraged in women. Now women are becoming active, becoming peacemakers, literally making peace. There are women who stay at home and make it a priority to work for peace; there are working women who make time in their evenings and at weekends; there are those who feel that it is such an urgent issue that they shelve their plans for the future in the hope that this way there will be a future. What we all share is the conviction that we must act now, and the hope that such action will be effective. The growing commitment to equal rights and opportunities has created a climate where women can find the courage to act on their ideas, their thoughts. With all the current problems in society, women cannot narrow down to one issue alone: our vision and insight makes us see the whole picture. Yes, we want a nuclear-free world, but we want also an end to violence, suffering and injustice. We want people to care more about themselves, about each other and about the planet. As women, we are following our instincts for survival. We are reacting to the threat of annihilation under governments that are considering genocide. The current movement is an expression of all our fear, and our determination to take our lives into our own hands. Joan Baez wrote in *Daybreak*, 'Part of the reason my fears play a minor role in my life now it that I have so many passions and commitments that terror is replaced and put aside.'

We are just beginning, of course. When we have ended the

nuclear threat, we must look at the continual failure of our societies to live in peace. We must evolve new ways of doing things; find ways to improve the quality of life for everyone alive on the planet. We want bread, and roses and dancing at the revolution too!

One woman who is active in the peace movement found that she was inspired to act when she came across this statistic: 1.7 per cent of the population make the decisions for the rest of us. And who are this 1.7 per cent? They are those MPs you voted for because they seemed the best of a bad lot. They are those MPs you didn't vote for. They are the generals. They are the ones who appear on Parkinson, the old men who tell us there have been no wars since the Second World War.

These men have now presented us with the ultimate deterrent: nuclear weapons. Weapons so powerful that they must never be used or we will all die, and our beautiful planet will be made uninhabitable forever. This is the logical conclusion to centuries of militarism: the perfect killing machine is one that kills everything and destroys all chance of life as we know it and as we love it. The nature of these weapons has changed many people's perceptions of the world. We cannot build for a future if our future is unlikely. We cannot pretend that our lives have meaning and purpose and value if they are to be snatched away from us at the arbitrary whim of a superpower driven by a vision of its own. Most of us would like to make our own decisions and the nuclear arsenal imperils this option. It makes us dispensable statistics. We are forced into a schizophrenic existence: we are asked to live as though planning for the rest of our lives, and, simultaneously, as though we may not be here tomorrow.

So we cannot accept their vision any longer. In the words of the bumper-sticker, 'It will cost the earth.' But we have a vision of our own. Not an illusion – we've had that, with heaven and the lies of a society which tells us that hard work will fulfil all our hopes and dreams. The saying, 'Where there's life, there's hope,' has a new and terrifying literalness for us in 1983. We begin to question the nature of the material rewards and unnamed fears on which our society is based. When we know that our lives are daily under threat, a threat which can only increase unless we ourselves stop it, we begin to say, 'no'.

It is a slow process, changing people's minds. It is painful, and often the systems seem too large or too strong. But we are the 98.3 per cent and we will be heard now.

On one of her visionary paintings, Monica Sjöö wrote, 'Women are rising with a force . . . older than the earth itself, and we will be free now, or no-one will survive.' It seems to many women that the way men have been running things for centuries has come to its own end. The patriarchs are trying now to out-threaten each other; and the protection they are promising us only increases our fears.

The visions that women evolve are very different. There are as many visions as there are women. Some of the common features are an absence of strife, a harmony with nature, an awareness of the seasons and the cycles of the earth, an acknowledgement of each person's worth. The symbols of these visions are also new. At Greenham we use the sign of the tree of life: in one badge it can be seen splitting a rock with its own natural growth force. There is the rainbow, which expresses the variety and colour and hope of our lives. Above all there is the web: the sign of the ancient women's skills of spinning and weaving, a spider's web that grows stronger as it is tested. The web also symbolises our linking and joining together. One of the most frustrating things for the police at Greenham actions is having to snip through wool and thread webs woven across the gates and fences.

It is all very down to earth, back to nature, to simplicity after centuries of mystifying religion and patriarchal power which have relegated women to inferior positions and glorified their passivity.

Women have earned 'respect' by becoming disempowered. Society and religion have found it convenient to define the good, healthy woman in mainly negative terms. The most glorious moment for women in the Christian religion was when Mary said, 'Be it unto me according to thy word.' Passive acceptance. Lie back and think of England. Men must work and women must weep. Moan ye and do nothing.

We do not want to do nothing. We want to work for our future. We want peace now. We cannot live without it. We cannot accept a status quo in which train robbers are imprisoned and rapists go free; in which those who plan to destroy our beautiful earth are given the power to do so, and those who protest are imprisoned.

At the trials of Greenham Common women on 15 November 1982, the women said:

> 'I cannot be bound over to keep the peace, because there is no peace.'
> 'My conscience is above the law: we are talking about genocide.'
> 'I live in anguish and agony.'
> 'I feel this baby kicking in my belly, and I know I could not look him in the face if I acted in any other way.'

Women are listening to their own thoughts after centuries of indoctrination and disempowering. At first these thoughts are faint, but they are growing clearer and clearer. Women are listening to their nightmares and the nightmares of their children. One woman told how she had had a dream, a vague feeling of women working and living together; she went to Greenham, and there were the women. She held a jumble sale of her 'things' and moved down there with them. Now she says, 'I've never felt better.'

The feeling that 'we may not be here tomorrow' has sparked many women into action. Why follow the role of the home-maker and provider when that whole lifestyle is under threat?

Here are some quotations from the newspapers:

Despite the various problems still to be solved, the Reagan administration is so determined to meet the December 1983 deadline that the Pentagon has decided to begin production of the missile *before their development and testing programmes are complete*. (21 November 1982: my italics)

A full-scale alert of a Soviet nuclear attack caused panic among defence officials here [Washington] yesterday . . . there had been a faulty computer reading . . . the counter order was quickly dispatched around the world and *everything returned to normal* (1979: my italics)

Four dead in MX missile test. (29 November 1982)

GLC reveals . . . the big bang plan. When asked why the GLC had decided to break so many years of silence, Councillor Carr (Hackney) said, 'I think the report shows the scale of the lunacy of the government's Civil Defence policies. If you ever want to prove that you are all going to die, you just have to read this report.'
(29 November 1982)

There is no need to elaborate: the threat is blatantly real, and all over the world women are responding to it. Women see other, ordinary women breaking the habit of silence to speak out in public, or blocking the way of military trucks and bulldozers, writing letters, starting up groups and even managing to keep their sense of humour with it.
(Ann Pettit, *Women for Life on Earth newsletter*, Autumn Solstice, 1982)

As the rewards of society are no longer attractive enough to make us conform, so the punishments too lose their effectiveness. This century has seen the suffragettes in prison and hunger striking; in the 1960s people were imprisoned for their belief in peace, and now it is happening again. Women from Greenham were imprisoned following the actions of March, the blockading of the Stock Exchange, and the August Action when we symbolically invaded the base. A week, or a fortnight in prison? One of the women, on release, said that the next task would have to be reforming the prisons. The spirit of the movement is vibrant and living.

Zen and the Art of Baby Carriage Maintenance

Aileen La Tourette

The phone gave its single sharp note as I replaced it, saying what the voice at the other end had said only in polite morse code. Oh, shit.

No it was worse than that. Phyllis Block had said what she hadn't said more in sorrow than anger. Much more. In sorrow and in her eighth month, when you haven't got the energy for anger.

No it was worse than that. Not only that a pregnant Phyllis Block was sorrowful and it was my fault. That little ring as the phone went back to its repose had jogged my memory or prodded it closer to the brink it was already nearing. What I remembered was that I had had a similar, a painfully similar conversation with P.B. at about this time last year. And that memory dragged in its wake all the further pitiful coincidences and glaring differences between last year, this time, and now. Glaring differences was exactly right; as if my face suddenly glared at me from the mirror, catching sight of my last year's face behind it. Radiant and ravaged; last year and this.

Well, perhaps not radiant. But in the terms of my face, that is according to its own lights, *radiant*. The odd thing is that last year at this time I was doing exactly what I'm doing now, and it couldn't have been more different.

I was alone then and I'm alone now. But the two alones are

different as the proverbial night and day; the difference between glaring and radiant. The seven alone nights of this week, last year, were radiant, and if the dawn wasn't exactly rosy-fingered, it wasn't rubber-gloved either. This year the nights glare. I sit in the same room and the night and I glare at each other through the window, then it moves inside and I try to escape by falling asleep by the fire. But every time I wake up it's still glaring. And if I do sleep soundly, it puts on a mask and glares right down into my dreams.

Last year. I spent the nights listening to music and reading. I even saw my guardian angel. The thoughts that follow that, from the reader, probably go something like UH-HUH; or UH-OH; or AHHhhh, with a dying fall. Anyway something inarticulately uneasy and disdainful. All I can say is that's the best description I can think of for this character, who's appeared twice now. Once she had a huge silver Afro that unfolded like a rose around her face; this time he was a tall, tanned (you could say golden-skinned, but I won't) youth with a tentative smile. He just stood by the living-room door smiling tentatively, you could say wistfully; then he was gone.

The fact that the visitor could take male or female form with equal conviction, and detachment, is what led me to conclude it was an angel. I have a selective memory for the Roman Catholic lore that was funnelled into my ears by black-robed funnels for sixteen years – and I always kind of liked angels. We used to say in first grade (aged six) through eighth (aged fourteen), 'Good Morning, Sister,' to the funnel, 'I salute your guardian angel.' We didn't actually *salute*. That was for the American flag. But it wouldn't be a bad idea. Imagine if everyone went around saluting angels. They'd have to form a special wing (no pun intended) of the CIA to investigate. They'd be bound to find out all angels are communist. (They *must* be.) Then they'd have to put all the spies and planes in the sky . . . what peace on earth.

Last year. I wasn't frightened by the appearance of my animus or whatever euphemism you prefer. He didn't stay long either. At the time I'd just come back from the USA where I'd visited my family and fallen in love with an old friend. So part of the week was spent in writing and receiving letters, while Ben interviewed psychologists in Germany. Onion skin can do a lot to keep you warm. Last year I had onion skin, angels, music, poetry and a conversation with Phyllis Block in the course of which she offered to lend me her baby carriage for my five-month-old son and I gratefully accepted.

Pram. In a state of ecstasy or drunk or high there's no such thing as England or America, except in the everyday sense in which they do exist. Which is one kind, one province of existence you might say. And a very provincial kind of existence they have, compared to, say, radiance. The doors of drunkenness and highness tend to open rather easily, with practice; and the doors of ecstasy to stick. But a baby carriage is a baby carriage and that's what this is. A perambulator remains one of those high glossy black jobs vaguely resembling the Queen's coach and properly perambulated by a nanny in a uniform in Hyde Park. This was just an ordinary friendly run-down old baby carriage, and as such I didn't pay it much attention.

I might say, as a point of information, that the angel produced no ecstasy. Nor was I drunk or high at the time of his appearance. It was a very low-key experience. This year, however, I have been visited by one of the more baleful demons during my sojourn. Sexless, voiceless, it has taken hold not by apparition but by possession. One way you can tell an angel; they keep their distance. This demon fastens on with claws and beak just as depicted in all the satanic literature. Not that I go in for satanic literature and as I said I haven't seen it. But I could draw you a picture, if I could draw.

Don't be disappointed by the name. I can hear an exasperated sigh already. Is *that* the kind of demon she means? That's all? The angel stuff was okay but what a letdown – *ordinary jealousy*?

Ordinary jealousy. I'd just spent a whole night writing a hate letter to Ben on the new baby-blue sheet we'd bought in a sale which I knew he liked and which we'd made love on the night before he left. THE NIGHT BEFORE. He'd left at six a.m. that morning to spend a week in France with Glenda Frankenstein.

What a lousy thing to do. The name, I mean. But that's nothing. At the time of which I'm speaking, to say I could've killed her is much too mild. I could have killed her slowly and with every attempt at solemnity, but I know fits of uncontrollable laughter would have overcome me as I carved up certain portions.

And then Ben. Aside from the phrases of darkness on the sheets, I sat slumped on the floor of his study in a drunken haze devising a plot for his destruction. In his study is some video equipment on loan from the University of London where he's completing a Ph.D. on laughter. Children's laughter, to be precise. My own laughter was not precisely childish as I envisioned myself taking an axe to the equipment, which takes up one-quarter of the room. There is an axe, too, in the basement; it came with the house. Lizzie Borden-like, I'd go at the stuff. Then I'd ring his supervisor at Bedford, very subdued and melancholic, the next morning.

'Hello? Dr Butterworth? I'm afraid – oh, this is Maya Truthmonger. I'm Ben Soulless's wife. Yes. Well . . . Dr Butterworth do you know about his drinking problem? No? Oh, that's just as well. It's good to know there are still people left who don't. It's just that – well – he tends to become a bit violent. And his latest victim – oh, no, thank you, Dr Butterworth, I'm as well as can be expected. No, Dr Butterworth, he's totalled the video equipment. I'm afraid you can't speak to him, Dr Butterworth. You see, he was so ashamed he ran away – I think to France –'

I figured it wouldn't really devastate him; on the other hand there would always be at least one person at Bedford College who'd believe he was a drunken maniac. A few more would just think I was. Either way, it wouldn't do him much good.

But I didn't. What did I do? I spent the first three days buying clothes. I had just made some money, and I made it rain through my fingers. The trouble with demons is, they *are* ordinary. Evil is banal; Hannah Ahrendt was right. I didn't chop up the video machines. I did drink myself silly every night and spend hung-over days trying on skirts and tops. I don't know whether the choice of separates was symptomatic of my divided personality or not. But I still have a long Indian skirt I haven't even worn.

The other two weekdays were pseudo-sane; I went to work. It was a good thing I did. But last year I hadn't, and I was glad to be alone, without feeling anything negative about Ben. What had happened?

In between, the world turned around. Or half-turned; what I faced now was an icy, chiselled profile. Last year I was in love with someone else as well as gently entwined with Ben and the children as well as . . . as well as unaware that someone I loved could founder could disappear could die, could even despair; and die. And earth's cold shoulder had been turned my way since then; since my oldest friend died.

Despair. Well you might say something else inarticulate and disbelieving about that. You might even be articulate, and right, but then again you can't possibly know and neither can I. But he went in for important outside-the-boundaries-of-America-and-England knowledge only when drunk; and that was a lot, during the last three years of his life.

Last year the world was whole, composed of a full quota of terrestrial and extra-terrestrial beings. This year there was nobody there, and Phyllis Block had just stopped herself from crying when I told her her baby carriage was a write-off.

So on Saturday I pushed the thing to a repair shop, *the* repair shop, and they looked and said Madam please remove it from the premises. Back to the premises of my own front hall where it had stood immobilised for the last three months – because Charlie was too big for it and anyway the springs didn't jounce him anymore and one wheel went for the gutter and the bonnet was hoist on its own petard – the hinge thing on the side stuck straight through it – so it was just taking up space in the front hall being used as a coat-rack and a library book holder and finger-painting receptacle.

Before that we used it plenty. And Charlie had plastered and muralled it with jam and milk and blackcurrant syrup and bits of cheese and apple. He had experimented and I had let it all harden into a permanent attraction. A permanent repulsion, by this time. And the canvas was going in the body of it as well. But Phyllis had used it for her other two kids. And her eight-months-pregnant voice wobbled as she said so.

I'd sort of poked it with a wet rag a few times while I was using it. As I was wondering whether I should do so again, and deciding that the gesture would only make me feel even more futile, the phone rang and it was Ben.

Who was away, by the way, by agreement. We were both meant to have a week away with friend. But my friend had backed out. So I had freely accepted, not *this* situation, but this situation; and my rage was unjustified, or unwarranted, or something. And Glenda had some claim to friendship as well and we had all Talked About It beforehand until we – or I – was green from you know-what and blue from shortness of breath. My smoking had suddenly jumped from one to two packs a day.

I told the voice on the phone it had a right to communicate with its children but not with me. When it persisted I told it to go shove itself up the nearest Glenda and hung up. I heard Charlie take the phone off the receiver again from upstairs. And I felt *calm*. For the first time in five days; calm.

This was the third or fourth phone call. The others had see-sawed, but dipped upwards of the toneless monosyllable and downwards of the piercing scream. The ugly side had mostly turned inwards. Now it was out and I felt clear-headed and empty and *light*. As I came down the stairs I saw the baby carriage ship-wrecked in the hall. I didn't think. Just as I didn't think why I felt restored. I just went into the kitchen and got a bucket and a cloth and some disinfectant. I went back later for a knife to scrape off the muck, and for a hammer and a screw driver and some screws.

I scrubbed the carriage, then I fiddled with the wheel. The hub-cap thing in the centre was loose, that was all. The bonnet was okay with a few replaced screws. Nothing could be done about the body; it was just old. But it would do; Phyllis could use it for at least the first few months of her baby's life.

I guess the angel was warning me. Not just harbinging someone else's death. Trying to gentle me into parting with a few cherished illusions without losing myself along with them. Like the illusion of proliferating love, a chain reaction that ended up in a pile-up. Sam. Whom I had left to his despair for Joey. Who had seen what lay ahead. Leaving Ben, and Glenda; whom I had punished for the terror of that bloodshot glaring eye that was my own fixed stare.

Which left the kids; and Phyllis. I got Charlie and Bert dressed and eased the carriage carefully down the stairs. It didn't exactly have that proud gleam, it was no perambulator; it was a function-ing ramshackle old baby carriage. We walked it home through the softly weeping evening.

A CATHOLIC EDUCATION PROVIDES A GIRL

AN IDEAL OF MOTHERHOOD....

PLENTY OF ROLE MODELS,
mostly young, beautiful, and dead

TWO DRESS REHEARSALS
FOR MARRIAGE
at First Communion and
confirmation

....ORIGINAL ASPIRATIONS

A SOUND GRASP OF MALE SUPREMACY

WITH...

A THOROUGH GROUNDING
IN BIOLOGY

ABORTION entails removing a living child from the womb, and smashing its skull with a hammer

If you vote Labour on Thursday, the RUSSIANS will walk into this country! PRIESTS will be tortured! NUNS interfered with! Churches sacked and looted! Our little ones forced into Precocious Knowledge of Life!

Mass gymnastics will be the order of the day! Abortion, birth control and euthanasia will be obligatory!

PRIESTS TORTURED?

NUNS INTERFERED WITH?

MASS GYMNASTICS?

......ASTUTE POLITICAL ADVICE

EXPERT HELP
FOR THE TROUBLED SOUL....

Now you'll feel a lot better if you run along and read 'The Hound of Heaven,' and join a Catholic youth club...

... and remember, there's Irish Dancing every Thursday at St Aloysius'

technically speaking there is no reason why a healthy woman should not have fifteen to twenty healthy babies.

MARRIAGE GUIDANCE
FROM QUALIFIED
COUNSELLORS.

© Jo Nesbitt, 1982.

A Woman Needs a God like a Fish Needs a Bicycle

Gail Chester

Having been born into an orthodox Jewish family whose religious practices I submitted to, willingly and unwillingly, until I was eighteen, I take rather a jaundiced view of feminists who embrace the supposed delights of religions, ancient and modern, in the relative freedom and maturity of adulthood. My experiences have not led me to think that Judaism is worse than any other religion, quite the reverse. As religions go, I feel it has more to offer than most. Its rituals at home and in the synagogue are more fun – designed to keep everybody involved. There are rational explanations for many of its restraints; it is much more interested in rewarding goodness than in punishing evil; and it doesn't give you an insurmountable spiritual handicap from birth – what point is there in struggling against original sin? Judaism is certainly no more patriarchal than any other religion and to claim otherwise is to fall for an updated version of anti-Semitic slander.

No, my objections to religion are not specific to Judaism; I believe that any religious practice is profoundly incompatible with the desire to achieve feminist revolution. I am against trying to update the established religions, to make them trendily relevant, and I am equally opposed to the manufacture of new synthetic religions, which attempt to give meaning to this plastic era. Additionally, I have particular criticisms of what some Jewish feminists are doing in attempting to reconcile Jewish ritual with feminism, as my understanding of why we organise as Jewish feminists is that we come together to fight against our oppression, as Jews and women, not to collude with it.

The only way you can defeat a patriarchal system is by exposing it for what it is, not by papering over the cracks and calling it something else. Renaming Stalingrad Volgograd didn't move it out of the USSR. Similarly pushing the frontiers of Europe hundreds of miles in each direction in the nineteenth century made no difference to the everyday life of the local inhabitants. They spoke the same language as before, ploughed the same fields, and continued to live in nation states ruled by despots.

An example of what concerns me comes from issue 7 of *Lilith – the Jewish Woman's Magazine* from the USA. Jane Litman, 'a feminist writer and Judaic scholar . . . [whose] particular interest is female-identified spirituality and ritual', writes:

> This Rosh Hashana I celebrated with a group of eight women – five loving thoughtful Jewish women and three loving thoughtful non-Jewish women. We read and sang outdoors, under an arbour of oak trees and danced until midnight the dances our mothers have danced with each other for three millenia. We blew the shofar and listened to its haunting melody fade into the soft darkness. We sang: henai mah tov u'mah nayim shevot achiot gam yachad – How good it is when sisters sing together.
>
> We drank wine and made blessings – blessed our mothers, ourselves, women who love other women, women working out ways to deal with men, men struggling to overcome their own sexism. We also blessed the wind, the sky, and Mother Earth. We wove a web of yarn in and out of our fingers, back and

forth across the circle, each time affirming our pride as women and our connection to the Eternal One, blessed be She. We read poetry – Hannah Senesh to Robin Morgan. We talked about the New Year, the new moon, and our pleasure in having old traditions to reform and rekindle. We finally broke up slowly, not wanting to leave the warmth we had made.

I suppose I felt for my service a similar feeling to that which male Hasidim feel after they dance and pray all night – a feeling of tremendous joy and oneness with the Creator . . .

I cannot pray in a place that is just a more subtle version of the scene in Mea Shearim. [Mea Shearim is an ultra-orthodox district of Jerusalem.]

The trouble is, what she describes is *not* Judaism, it's any female-centred spirituality. Anything I would recognise as practising Judaism must remain a 'more subtle version of Mea Shearim'. Reinterpreting Judaism in this way is profoundly disrespectful to those very ancestors with whom people like Jane Litman claim solidarity, and whose achievements they aspire to emulate.

Either Judaism is a particular set of religious beliefs or it is nothing. Trying to redefine it in another (anti-patriarchal) way is to play into the hands of the anti-Semites. It is to say, 'All right, I'm stuck with the label "Jew" which you have put on me, but in reality, left to myself, I can't relate to it because Judaism is old-fashioned/irrelevant/patriarchal. However I must continue to relate to something called Judaism, because you have left me no alternative, and so I will invent this totally different thing and say, "Look I'm proud of it".'

But that still doesn't make it Judaism. If you are so proud of Judaism, why change it, why want to wrench it so completely from its roots that it is no longer recognisable as the original? A

Jewish feminist friend told me recently that she believed that anything a Jewish woman chose to define as Jewish feminist ritual was indeed that, because she was in control of her own definitions, and was refusing to have them defined for her by the patriarchy. This is all very well in terms of the pro-woman line – supporting women in whatever they do in order to survive. It is false consciousness to call it Judaism.

Women (and men) born into a Jewish background are as much victims of seventies' and eighties' alienation, the search for meaning, as anyone else. It is not surprising that one option for people seeking spiritual solace is to return to a ready-made ritual, maybe souping it up to salve their radical consciences. Another solution, clutched at by both Jews and non-Jews, is to formulate entirely new rituals to fit the image of a religion. Some go off the rails entirely, abandon any thought of changing the world and depart to change their heads, in India, South Korea or West Coast, USA. But others sincerely believe that the revolution can be brought about by creating new religions, harnessing womenergy and pursuing matriarchal deities. They are more insidious as they hang about, diverting energy, trying to convince the rest of us that we are mistaken, intolerant, missing a Beautiful Experience, or just plain old lost souls, if we don't want to join in.

All peoples, since time immemorial, have created their gods in their own image, and the matriarchalists are no different. But isn't it more comforting to find admirable women to revere who really lived or are alive today than to be consoled by the productions of one's own fertile imagination? I would find it more depressing than uplifting to consider that there might not be enough genuine female achievement to admire, so that I and my friends had to invent some.

At particular periods in history, the need to invent gods becomes overwhelming. In times of uncertainty 'god' is actually the need to provide an answer for everything. Conventional wisdom says that atheists need to be completely rational, have 'scientific' answers to all the mysteries of the universe and leave nothing unexplained. Whereas precisely the opposite is true – I can readily accept that there are many elements of existence which are inexplicable. Inventing god still doesn't explain them, it just stops people needing to search for the truth. God is not truth, god is cosy, a comfort in times of trouble.

Alternatively god is punitive, or at best couldn't care less. To advocate religion is to encourage passivity, to accept that the vicissitudes of fate are beyond our control. Secure in the knowledge that the operation of our planet is in the hands of this god, alternately benign and malevolent, we have no need to question the cause of what are usually referred to as 'natural disasters'. We accept that this is god throwing the celestial dice, if not a temper tantrum.

Yet for every disaster that is truly natural, the result of an unpredictable seismic shock, for example, there are another dozen which are the result of human greed or vanity – the careless interference with the ecosystem which causes deserts to encroach and forests to die, rivers to flood and crops to diminish. Neither is it divine will that the majority of such disasters should happen in the Third World. Until people stop needing to believe in a god to assuage their guilt or facilitate their acceptance of the inequitable allocation of the earth's resources, they will not be able to see clearly which 'acts of god' are the random assaults of nature and which are the results of human oppressors' profound disrespect for other people and the earth.

Revolutionary change and *any* form of religious practice are profoundly incompatible. How can you intend to change the world and still expect to give up your free will to something beyond your control? If you are against hierarchies and élites, how can you participate in practices which accept belief in a supreme extra-terrestrial being of either or no gender, which employs earthly intermediaries (of either gender) to interpret its message for you, and guide, nay lead, you in the paths of righteousness?

Most of us have to fight for the right for our argument to be heard in the market-place where ideas are exchanged. How can we compete with those who claim divine inspiration, irrefutable knowledge, from the highest authority? Such people are normally labelled 'megalomaniac' or 'schizophrenic' and locked up. Sometimes in our society we send them to seminary for a few years instead, and then let them wander round in fancy dress. We pay them great respect and call them Vicar, or Rabbi, or Imam. I do not understand how people who aspire to radical change, especially feminists, can train to be rabbis (or any other sort of religious guru). I am staggered by the arrogance of it, by their lack of awareness of the incongruity between wanting to be a leader, claiming to know better than all the rest of us, and supporting the struggle for the egalitarian society we want to bring about.

Religion is about conformity, obedience and failure to challenge authority or the status quo. A religious framework provides space to ask questions only within the boundaries of the accepted orthodoxy. It produces an authoritarian yet quiescent environment, the very antithesis of a climate of rebellion. It will never encourage the liberation of women and we comply at our peril.

Hard times are upon us; we hear a lot more talk than we used to about the need for elevated role models – women as MPs as well as religious leaders, and about the need for resources inside ourselves – back to the godhead and spirituality, the benefits of prayer and feminist tarot. These are counsels of despair. They may be the only realistic tactics for surviving the economic crisis and the threat of nuclear war, but they are not a strategy for feminist revolution.

'I used to live in a long stretchy street . . .'

Jeanette Winterson

I used to live in a long stretchy street with a town at the bottom and a hill at the top. My mother and father walked arm in arm down the street to the church: always the same, six o'clock crashing through the letterbox, a headscarf, a Bible, a pair of clean shoes, clean-shaven father, scented mother.

Years ago my mother childless, longing, prayed to God for a sign and found her own particular star. She followed it in faith, and came to a dingy cot in a shabby orphanage and a child with too much hair.

She said, 'This child is mine from the Lord.'

So she took the baby home and washed away its parents' sin and plotted a new life for the child. A missionary, a servant of god. A blessing.

The child had nits, the child had dreams. At night the child screamed, but the mother saw that the demons were jealous of her prize and told the child to praise the Lord. And the child did.

Years passed and the child preached to the people in the might of the Spirit. Many and more filled the church, consumed by Pentecostal fire. We sang and clapped and each night the child underlined her Bible and prayed that the devil might be vanquished. The mother nodded, the father smiled.

They shared their bed but never their bodies. 'What need?' said the mother, when their souls were wedded in Christ.

Then, the Word became flesh, I saw God in another woman and I loved her. I who had no teaching in guile could not hide and saw no need to do so. Did not David and Jonathan love?

I am haunted by my mother's scent, my mother's twisted face, my father's silence and my own dry hands holding a Bible, refusing to believe that my love and that book were separated by the chaos of damnation.

I remember the nits, I was crawling with nits, but the elders of the church would cleanse me as the mother had cleansed me before. A lurking demon but the mother would not let the devil snatch her child.

Easter time and on the hill at the top of the stretchy street they drove a cross into the earth. Huge and black it was. The child saw the cross and on a wild night ran to it clung to it and prayed to God her friend to take away the demon nits and leave her free from pain. The hill lay black and trenched, ditches from the war. The child was running, running, but the image lay in the distance. Wood on wood nail on nail. It began to rain, the child thought it was raining blood. And she drenched in black blood.

At home the mother prayed and drew comfort from the Bible.

The father visited the sick. At night they talked in low voices, the mother bitter, defeated. She had been bidden by the Lord to search the room of the child. She found letters. Intense, white-hot hungry letters from the loved one to the child.

The child lay still in a narrow bed and cried to God to forgive her but she could not forgive herself because the loved one had branded her on both hands.

The mother said, 'You are a child of the devil.'

A hand was nailed by God; a hand was nailed by the devil.

The feet were nailed by the loved one. Through the side, the spear flung by those who thought themselves betrayed. On her head the thorns of the mother. For years the taste of vinegar remained.

When Hitler Returns: The Impossibilities of Being a Jewish Woman

The bittersweet character of my relationship with Judaism was crystallised in 1977, when I had to write a dissertation in the third year of my social anthropology degree. Practically everybody seemed to choose a topic that was a personal baptism of fire, a *rite de passage* into the outside world, a final attempt at self-analysis before the gates of academe clanked shut behind them.

I was no exception to this. An intellectual fancy of linking Mary Douglas's thesis in *Purity and Danger*[1] concerning Jewish dietary laws with the notion that dietary preferences and sexual choice are symbolically parallel, led me to reread the Old Testament looking at the laws of family purity. This proved so extraordinary that I abandoned all anthropological pretension, talked my way into Jews' College Library and settled down to vindicate my gradual divorce from the religion of my birth.

Naturally, it didn't quite work like that. The more I read, the more I was repelled, the more I was fascinated. Instead of clearing Judaism and the associated guilt and confusion out of my system, my work merely compounded it, multiplying the complications in my identity to the nth degree. And those preoccupations led to this essay.

This seems as good a place as any to point out that I do not claim to be the world's leading authority on Jewish women. I also recognise the bias in my reading of various laws and attitudes. I concede that there is much that I have not read and no doubt plenty in what I have read that I have misunderstood. I put forward merely my opinion and beliefs based on several months of intensive study. My sources were the Bible, the most important commentaries on it, and the major codifications of Jewish law as well as scores of Jewish scholarly works. The relationship of these codes of law to Jewish women's everyday practice is complex. While many practising Jews observe them only selectively, their influence remains subtle and pervasive and extends even to those whose observance is minimal.

One of the major problems of being a Jewish woman is that culturally, socially and religiously, such a creature doesn't exist. A person is a Jew by serving God through the fulfilment of the 613 *mitzvot* (commandments) in the Pentateuch. Women, however, are 'excused' from most of these on the grounds of their 'physical infirmity' and their inability to keep to a regular timetable because of their commitment to children. Consequently, women take little part in the religion and are also debarred from study. 'Whosoever teaches his daughter Torah teaches her lasciviousness,' says the Talmud, thus at a stroke denying women the chance to attain *olam habo* (future life), a state achieved mainly through points gained for pious behaviour and religious study. Women can get into heaven only on their husbands' or fathers' tickets. The modern reform and liberal strands of Judaism which permit the ordination of women rabbis are a minority among Jews and are seen by the majority as simply breaking the rules.

In fact, the Talmudic pronouncement sets in motion a circular argument of epic proportions. Since a Jew without learning is incomplete, a woman can never be a complete Jew. Because she has no learning she is stupid, therefore she cannot be trusted with anything important, therefore she must be kept away from the holy

Torah and the chance to gain knowledge. The Talmud also says, 'Better the words of the Torah were burned than put into a woman's keeping.' Since religious Jews throughout history have chosen to die rather than desecrate the Torah, and since a central tenet of Jewish law has it that life must be preserved at all costs, it's clear how deep this feeling runs.

Oh well, so much for religion, what about the rest of life, one might say. Unfortunately in strictly orthodox Judaism, there isn't any rest of life. Society, ethnicity, culture – for the minority of Jews who follow all the rules, the religion itself is all of these things. Nothing, but nothing, exists outside this supremely intellectual and cerebral pale, except the ambiguous sexuality of women.

The key to women's position within Judaism lies, as with so much else, in Genesis.[2] The Hebrew word for man is *ish* and for woman, *ishah*. However, the *Encyclopaedia Judaica* maintains that these words do not stem from the same root. *Ish* comes from *enosh* (mankind, human beings) whereas *ishah* is derived from a word meaning to be compatible (Genesis 2:18, 'And the Lord God said, it is not good that man should be alone; I will make him a helpmeet for him'). Thus the Jewish view of woman is that she was 'created to serve man as a suitable helper . . . and her essence as a human being is linked with her function as companion to the male' (Talmud again).

In fact, Judaism goes on to formalise this right through its structure, like the letters in a stick of rock, aided and abetted by the punishments meted out by God in the Fall. Adam is cursed by God to a life of hard labour, but the curse of Eve is to be bound forever by her sexuality (Genesis 3:16, 'Unto the woman he said, I will greatly multiply thy sorrow and thy conception; in sorrow thou shalt bring forth children; and thy desire shall be to thy husband and he shall rule over thee'). Since it was Eve's sexuality that brought about the Fall, and since this same sexuality is a daily reminder of it, the law makers felt justified in regarding women merely as walking sex-drives, carnality in motion.

Cutting across this distaste, to put it politely, for female sexuality as a constant reminder of the Fall and ever-present threat to the current culture and religion, is the helpmeet aspect of the affair. For orthodox Jews the most important commandment in the book, because it is written twice, is that of procreation (Genesis 1:28, 'Be fruitful and multiply, and replenish the earth and subdue it'). Like the vast majority of *mitzvot*, however, this is aimed only at those who do the subduing (men), not at those who are subdued (women). Women's role in the affair is to be the vehicles for producing extra souls to worship God. According to relatively modern interpretations, a couple's duty is done when they have replaced themselves in the world with a son and a daughter, but piety suggests that they should have as many children as possible. It has been said that to the orthodox Jewish man, his bride represented the soil in which his seed was to be planted, the means by which he could secure the offspring which represented his immortality.

Aside from the conception of the children that the *mitzvah* demands (and the inability of a woman to conceive brings her a swift divorce), the act of sexual intercourse sees women acting as helpmeets in the avoidance of an important negative commandment, *hash-hatat zera* (the improper emission of seed). This refers not only to the avoidance of masturbation (male masturbation is considered by the law makers equivalent to murder as, among other things, it violates Isaiah 1:15, 'Your hands are full of blood') but also to the tenet that the only proper place for semen is inside the vagina of a woman. Many traditional Jewish writers see intercourse as cathartic for men, cleansing the body of its fullness and so on. However, the issue of semen out of place, such as masturbation and nocturnal emission, makes a man unclean, due to the loss of potential life in the form of 'wasted' seed.

Women's position within all this is highly ambivalent. Semen properly discharged into women is all right – when it leaks out again as post-coital discharge it is defiling (to men). Because the mere touch of a woman's body, even in total innocence, might lead to impure thoughts it is considered indecent. Women are alluring in order to make sure that men observe the commandments but this makes them a potential threat and temptation to every man they meet in the street. Many very orthodox men will not shake hands with a woman and most will avoid looking at her at all. A couple of years ago in New York, where the best and cheapest camera shop is run by very orthodox Jews, I had the bizarre experience of being shown how to operate a highly complex camera by a man who stared at the floor throughout the entire operation. Even the person who took my money wouldn't look at me.

Because women's sexuality is seen to be so unpredictable and potent it is set about with a myriad of rules and restrictions. These refer not only to general standards of modesty and decorum such as cropping the hair and the correct length of skirts and sleeves but also enter into the most intimate relationships between men and women. 'Woman is dangerous, not only because she herself lacks virtue, but still more because she rouses in man a desire stronger than his will and judgment.'[3] Get a man alone in a room with a woman – even one he's married to – and goodness only knows what will happen. So there have to be rules to make sure that he stays on top – both figuratively and literally.

After all, it is he who is doing the subduing. In Hebrew the word *ba'al* means master, husband, and to have sexual intercourse. Since intercourse must also be masterful, only the missionary position is really kosher, as it were. The Shulchan Aruch[4] asserts that this position is the most modest (he can see least of her body) and that 'he underneath and she above him is considered an impudent act, both at the same level a pervert act' – not least because they do not include the domination that *ba'al* implies. There is some shaky evidence to suggest that entry from behind is okay and this seems plausible, since he is still in some sense on top and she is arguably in a position of servility.

Other mechanics of sexuality are equally complicated. Husband and wife must never see each other naked – and four inches of exposed female flesh which is normally covered constitutes nakedness. The kissing of a woman's genitals violates Leviticus 11:43, 'Ye shall not make yourselves detestable.' A married man can touch his penis only to urinate, while unmarried men must never touch theirs at all.

On top of this comes the fear (and I use the word advisedly) of menstruation. The name for the laws surrounding this have, in my view, a terrifying name: *tacharat hamishpachah*, the purity of the family. With the onset of her menstrual period a woman becomes *niddah*, a word which implies impurity or separation. During her period and for several days afterwards a woman is defiling not only in intimate terms (no intercourse or touching is allowed), but also to the world at large. Everything she sits on, sleeps on and so forth is also rendered unclean. A woman is generally *niddah* for twelve days, after which she goes for immersion in a *mikveh* (ritual pool) and is essentially reborn through this monthly baptism, becoming clean for her husband again.

Before this return to the real world a lot of silliness goes on. For example, menstruating women are discouraged from eating at the same table as their husbands unless some unusual object is placed between them. If a menstruating woman wants to put something down in front of her husband she must do so in an unusual manner – backhandedly is suggested. There are involved instructions in the Shulchan Aruch explaining to men what they must do if their wives start to menstruate during intercourse. A woman who has the misfortune to bleed habitually during intercourse will find herself divorced and unable to remarry.

An endless amount of apologetic has been written about *tacharat hamishpachah*: how it stops women from being used like prostitutes, makes married life exciting and so on. However, the establishment view takes us, yet again, back to both the Fall and Isaiah 1:15. Through her temptation, Eve brought about the death of Adam, thus shedding his blood, so along with the sorrow and the conception, she is punished through her blood.

Blood, for observing Jews, is the mystery of life, the libation given to God in sacrifice. The dietary ban includes the words, 'Only be sure that thou eat not the blood: for the blood is the life; and thou may not eat the life with the flesh'.[5] Consequently, when eating the flesh of women through intercourse men can't have the blood as well. And this isn't any old blood, but is life-blood, though transmuted in a sense into death-blood, since its very existence suggests that all that precious semen *was* discharged in vain, as conception has not taken place. Furthermore, intercourse during menstruation would probably only serve to waste more of the wonderful stuff, since conception at such a time is relatively unlikely. Leviticus 20:18 suggests that menstruous intercourse be punished with excommunication.[6]

In order to make sure that she is free of menstrual blood before she goes to the *mikveh*, a woman must examine herself at least twice a day for a week. It has been suggested that the encouragement of this is a veiled validation of female masturbation. The Mishnah puts it thus: 'The hand that often-times makes examination is, among women, praiseworthy, but among men – let it be cut off.' However, this can also be interpreted as a warning to men not to touch their wives in dubious places, particularly when there is a threat of menstrual defilement.

At the same time the laws do recognise that women have other than procreative sexual needs. The *mitzvah* of *onah* orders men to have intercourse with their wives at least once a month, as well as after the return from the *mikveh*. Attitudes to female homosexuality appear to be tolerant too. Male homosexuality is a major crime, punishable by death. Lot offered his virgin daughters to the mob in Sodom rather than allow it access to the strange men who were visiting him so that so vile a thing as male homosexuality could be avoided.[7] There is no corresponding prohibition of female homosexuality. The law is left tantalisingly ambiguous – women may sleep together, for example.

However, all these apparent 'advantages' work against women within the context of Judaism. What is denied men – who are the centre of the culture and religion – is allowed to women, those dangerous sexual beings on the fringes of civilisation, who can never quite be trusted not to turn a quick trick of some sort. Better, then, that they masturbate or satisfy each other's sexual needs, relieving their frustrations with their own kind and thus allowing themselves to present a pure image within the context of home and family. Any strategy they choose to deal with their assumed constant state of sexual readiness is self-defeating; it is the sexuality itself which is dangerous within the context of the religion.

Having got this far, it was clear to me that Judaism was essentially, at its very roots, anti-feminist. As a social system traditional Judaism keeps women in the servants' quarters. In complicated ways the religion regards women as existing only to support men. There's not much comfort for a woman there, I thought.

Most of my research had been a complete revelation to me. Nearly all of it was totally outside my own ambit, although certainly there is a large number of orthodox women around to whom all this stuff is to a greater or lesser extent relevant on a day-to-day basis. I had rejected the religious trappings of Judaism some years previously and this had been fortified by my now long-finished involvement in Zionist socialism, a subject covered in another contribution to this book. When I thought of religion I saw it in sentimental terms – lighting Sabbath candles, making benedictions over bread and apples and honey at New Year, getting drunk at Passover. On the rare occasions when my attendance in synagogue was mandatory I enjoyed the singing and the anthropologist in me was constantly delighted by the rituals. It was like observing a primitive tribe in the field, something I was never likely to do in reality. I felt superior but with inside knowledge.

I also realised that I knew a lot more about the position of women in the classical tradition of Judaism than most other people did. While I had previously recognised that women had little importance within the religion – the whole structure of the services, the synagogue and the rituals underlined that – I had not recognised the lengths to which this was taken. The statement in Leviticus[8] that a mother is *niddah* for seven days after the birth of a male and fourteen days after that of a female child meant to me, despite everything I read to the contrary, that females were in some way inherently defiling. Small wonder, then, that one of the first benedictions observing Jewish men make upon waking is one thanking God for not making them women!

It struck me that I just couldn't go on upholding any vestige of the religion of my birth. Anyway, it surely no longer wanted anything to do with me. My research had turned me into a *tagid*, a heretic, a person with a fund of knowledge about the intricacies of the religion but who then chose to shun it.

Logically, then, this should have been the end of the story. I should have stopped defining myself as Jewish, thrown away my little book of psalms and my Chaim Potok novels, forgotten how to make *tsimmis* and *matzah* balls – in short, tossed the whole sexist patrimony in the bin – and got on with assimilating myself even further into the British majority. After all, although I had amassed, by some extraordinary means of molecular chemistry, a large number of Jewish friends, I had never tried specifically to achieve this. Non-Jews often thought I was Italian or Cypriot but never guessed I was Jewish. I didn't live in a Jewish area, I had no intention of getting married – I could sink without trace. It was stupid to retain silly attachments to the cooking and the ceremonies – truly the chocolate bobbles on the whipped cream on the icing on the cake – when the basic structure was so distasteful. Nothing, in theory, could have been simpler. In theory.

However, within me there was a small but persistent voice which wasn't having any of this. The voice was that of Sarah Kahn, the heroine of Arnold Wesker's play *Chicken Soup with Barley* – by far the best portrayal of a strong, mixed-up Jewish woman that I know – and it was saying, 'You want me to move to Hendon and forget who I am?'

Sarah Kahn became my heroine in 1969, when I was fourteen and studying modern English literature at school. Brought up to revere the unexpected heroism of East End Jews when they defended their district against Mosley's Blackshirts in the Battle of Cable Street in 1936, I found everything I wanted in this marvellous play. Jews – and, indeed, Jewish women – could be fighters, communists, heroes. Sarah Kahn's view of communism – 'Love comes now. You have to start with love. How can you talk about socialism otherwise?' – still remains at the basis of my views – tempered with large doses of the Jewish Russian-American anarchist Emma Goldman, a real-life Sarah Kahn if ever there was one.

At the end of *Chicken Soup with Barley* Sarah's friends and family, horrified by events in Hungary in 1956, try to get her to give up her beliefs. She answers with the comment about Hendon. 'If the electrician who comes to mend my fuse blows it instead, so I should stop having electricity?' Somebody has got to go on caring, or else the whole world will disintegrate. She will go on fighting and caring, not least because she can't do anything else. Brotherhood (sic) will survive crises in the Communist Party.

In many ways Sarah Kahn is the ideal Jewish woman. Big,

fierce, capable, exhausted, perfectionist, supremely sacrificial, manic-depressive, she will go on fighting, even though she knows she is going to lose. She will even fight for things which in themselves aren't worth fighting for, just in case the fact of her having battled on their behalf imbues them with a new sense of purpose and realism (and beauty and light). Feed the world with tea and chicken soup and maybe it will learn to love not only the giver but also what she stands for.

On rereading *Chicken Soup with Barley* recently it was almost frightening to discover how closely I resembled Sarah Kahn – and, by extension, how closely my character fitted to a particular 'type'. All the elements of sacrifice, capability, enthusiasm, perfectionism and the rest of it are lined up in my psyche like targets in a shooting range. My sense of martyrdom and history is heavily pronounced. Faced with the impossible, the inescapable, the unconquerable – both at work and in my personal and emotional life – I go on hitting away at it until it's done.

It's total anathema to me to say 'no'. The bigger the request or crisis, the greater the challenge and drain on mental resources, the more difficult refusal becomes. Hand in hand with this goes my bossiness, my inability to sit still and watch apathy and inefficiency gum up the works. I can hardly bear to let people muddle through in their own way. Along with this too, though it hardly needs saying, goes a highly developed technique of breast-beating, self-analysis and self-criticism. Nothing, but nothing, is ever so good that it can't be improved. There's never a question of sitting still.

But, unlike Sarah Kahn, who appears never to consider this problem, I have a further reason for refusing to move away from my roots and forget who I am. When I was a child, my mother strongly disapproved of my having non-Jewish friends. No doubt at the back of her mind was the fear that if I got used to running around with non-Jews I might – God forbid – wind up marrying one. However, she chose to voice her objections in a different and much more frightening way, and one which will never stop being a major influence on my life. Which of them, she asked, would hide me when Hitler returns?

When Hitler returns, mark you, not 'if'. It wasn't just that Hitler was the bogeyman of my generation, like Napoleon had been for English children at the beginning of the nineteenth century. Hitler had been before in a variety of forms – various czars of Russia, Roman emperors and Spanish Inquisitors to name but a few – and his evil spirit was hardly likely to have been laid to rest forever in a German bunker. It wasn't a case, then, of if Hitler got you, it was a case of when.

Hitler's last reincarnation in Germany had proved a dire warning. The horror of all those people who genuinely thought that they were thoroughly German being carted off to die because it suddenly transpired that their grandmother was Jewish. All those people who did know they were Jewish but who thought that their financial or social power was enough to protect them. They felt needed, their assimilation was complete. They had sunk without trace into the German people.

They had moved to the suburbs, in fact, and forgotten who they were until Hitler reminded them. Hindsight, history and, later, my mother, were acutely aware of their fatal error. As a friend put it to me years after I had internalised this incessant scrutiny of my acquaintances to ascertain their motives – it doesn't matter what you do to make yourself acceptable, you'll still wind up being turned into a lampshade.

It was this fatalism that led me back to Sarah Kahn. Not just that there was no point in trying to forget who you were, because there would always be some sweet soul around who would be happy to remind you, but also that fighting to change circumstances was a historical imperative. Unless we learn who we are and what we are, shock will be added to all the other horrors when they come to take us away. I can think of nothing worse. Unlike Jewish men,

Jewish women have no outward signs of their ethnicity. The scars are all inside.

It's my belief that there isn't a Jew alive, be she religious, atheistic or betraying her roots, who isn't reacting to the Holocaust. It sets you against the rest of the world and then twists your guts. I'll fight and I'll fight – and then I'll lose. I'll accept any old rubbish the world flings at me and struggle to make it into a garden because it's the only way – and it's impossible. And I'd just better get on with it now, because when Hitler returns it will be a whole lot worse. Grim fatalism is a very Jewish disease.

There are any number of Jews who disagree with this theory: I've stopped defining myself as Jewish so I have ceased to be it/who cares anyway?/it'll never happen here. To them I would answer: firstly, the vast majority of German Jews reckoned it would never happen to them either. Secondly, whatever you say, you haven't lost the eternal chip on your shoulder – why am I alive? My co-religionists were decimated forty years ago and who the hell am I? You think that by stopping caring, by forgetting who you are, by moving away, you will stop Hitler returning? If it was all that easy he would never have existed in the first place.

It is waiting for Hitler's return, then (and, unlike Godot, this one is going to show up), that has prevented me from losing my Jewish identity entirely. At the same time it has made me to a greater or lesser extent suspicious of non-Jews. It has made me bossy and efficient, desperate to stay in control of all situations – if I hand the reins to someone else, will they steer the cart towards the gas chambers? It has made me set impossible standards for my friends, a thousand hurdles to leap and tasks to perform to prove themselves.

Conversely, it has made me very outgoing, seeking friends everywhere, trying to woo them – maybe this one will turn out to be a protector, someone I can rely on. I need a network of support to survive. It has turned me into an emotional exhibitionist, because I have nothing more to fear.

At the same time it has made me reluctantly tolerant of a lot of things and attitudes that I would – and do – otherwise despise. Sometimes on Saturdays I would go to north-west London and be moved to tears by the aching kinship I felt with what I termed the bigoted blue rinses of Golders Green. They go to synagogue, gossiping and feeling pious in equal proportions, finding safety in their passive ignorance. On every point, social and political, we would disagree. Yet I feel I understand something of the insecurities that make them tick, something of the forces that have led them to their materialistic and ostentatious solutions.

This is paralleled by my visits to Stamford Hill, where the most orthodox Jews live, the people who really practise the religion in all its manifestations. Intellectually and politically I could hardly be more at variance with anybody than I am with the pale, knicker-bockered men with ear-locks who walk the streets in their wide, fur-trimmed hats. I consider their way of life repressive and oppressive. But still I find myself admiring their honesty as they stride about wearing their faith and their identity on their sleeves. Their wives trot behind, bewigged, tired, permanently pregnant, endlessly symbolic (women walk behind men partly so that the men will not be moved to lustful thoughts by the sight of the swaying form in front, and partly in recognition of the *ba'al* relationship). But they too are my kindred, in a way that many non-Jewish feminists, say, are not.

All this could be interpreted as a very sorry state of affairs. Poor old Maureen, trapped by history, can't get out properly into the brave new world. What she needs is a quick bit of therapy, drama games, learn to trust others. Then she could chuck all that Jewish guilt in the dustbin and concentrate on the rest of life.

But while it's true that being Jewish would appear to be a multi-faceted bondage, and a lot more complicated underneath than first appearances suggest, I really don't want to get away. Leaving aside for the moment my conviction that it's not possible to make a complete break, there's also the pride that accrues from belonging to a special group, even if it is an oppressed and oppressive religion and culture. There's the idea, prevalent in feminist thinking, that women should accept that they are different and work through that to a position of strength and self-acceptance, rather than trying to get on in the world by aping the opposition.

In other words, if women are to be proud that they're gay, proud that they're Black, then they can also be proud that they're Jewish. Unfortunately it doesn't, from my angle, look that simple. For one thing, there's the idea that since it's all so patri-archal there's nothing in it of value at all and it can be safely ditched without regret. For another, there's all the confusion on the left about Israel, with the erroneous idea that all Jews are Zionists and all Jews support Begin therefore all Jews are right-wing therefore . . . The path of righteousness passes very close to the edge of the slippery slope in any number of places.

This, I feel, is not least due to the fact that a large proportion of non-Jews, when they come to consider Jewish people, are also full of guilt about the Holocaust, and it often pulls them in odd direc-tions. We all ought to be banding together to work our way through it. Instead we're all either sitting about doing nothing or else putting all our energy into forgetting about it altogether.

For me, then, the pressures of being a Jewish woman are many and various. It's impossible to feel any kinship with or affection for a religion that's so sexist (different but equal just doesn't hold up at all here) but at the same time it's impossible not to. It's impossible not to feel some sort of solidarity with other Jews while knowing that I'm at complete odds with the vast majority of the Jewish community. It's impossible to regard non-Jews without a fair degree of caution but at the same time I realise that I should be bigger than that. It's impossible to separate out those characteristics of my Jewish friends that I like because they're interesting from the feeling that their ethnic identity is a major attraction. It's amusing how often I or my friends show especial interest in a certain play or book or film because it's on a Jewish topic or is about Nazism or something similar. The fascination of fear.·

Furthermore, it's impossible to write this essay without the nagging doubt that it will be rejected because it's about Jews, or accepted because it's about Jews, or disregarded because it's not some comprehensive voice of all Jews at all times. British society would feel happiest if all Jews could be lumped together under a single heading, much like textbook West Indians or Asians or Irish people.

A stereotype and a neat solution. If Jews stopped being paranoid and neurotic about being Jewish, we'd be more accepting, says British society. Oh, yes, and why should I fall for that one? My prickliness, mate, is one of my tools for survival. Nobody else gets told that her life would be easier if she forgot who she was and moved to the suburbs.

Being a Jewish woman, then, in my view, is an impossibility, an inevitability and a cause for celebration. It's a kind of handicap and a kind of advantage (I've been forced to think through a number of issues which most people can conveniently forget). Being a Jewish feminist is a mass of contradictions. Trying to change the world while being convinced that, inevitably, one day Hitler will return is a nonsense. Being a Jewish woman puts forward a lot of sticky questions and provides very little in the way of answers. Forgetting about it and going away doesn't work.

Despite all this, I will never stop feeling that standing up and being counted on the basis of my ethnicity is a good thing. It's when we decided that being Jewish is something shameful and too difficult to deal with, and consequently shove it to the back of the cupboard, that we compound our problems. By facing them we may yet stop playing games of victims versus oppressors and emerge from it all as better people.

The Shepherdess and the Blooming Goats

A Woman's Eye View of the Ordained Ministry

Kate McIlhagga

'The God of all Grace, who called you to the Christian faith and service, confirm and strengthen you with the Holy Spirit and keep you faithful to Christ all your days.'

I lifted my hands from my son's head and he grinned at me and at his father standing beside me, as we conducted a recent confirmation service.

I had been told what a privilege it was to share the most meaningful occasions in life – the rites of passage – baptism, confirmation, marriage, communion and burial. I had never imagined what joy it could bring and how drained I could become.

When I stand among the crumpled orders of service and the confetti in an empty church, reeking not of incense but of perfume splashed on for high days and holidays, I experience the loneliness of the long-distance preacher. It has all washed up to and over me and out through the door into the street and I am left standing. It is after these events – the funeral or the wedding – that I find it most difficult to go home and face the unwashed breakfast dishes, the preparation of the next meal and the demands for dinner money, clean socks and sponsor forms. No wonder the clergy need a wife! I have a husband who is also a minister.

To be a woman and a priest is to experience the fulfilment of being obedient to God's call. To be a married woman and a minister is to know that God works not in some rarified realm of spirituality far from mundane things like wet nappies and Genesis belting forth from all corners, but in the very centre of those things, in everyday life. Someone said: 'God likes matter – he invented it.' It is in the material things that God is to be found. I see no division between the sacred and the secular, between work and worship, religion and politics. If this is God's world then everything in it relates to God – even the political infrastructures of our society. A gathering for worship must spill over into service in our everyday lives. Our everyday lives give God worth every time a hungry child is fed, a lonely person visited, or a joy shared. I refuse to split myself, or others, or life itself for that matter, into boxes labelled physical/mental/spiritual for the use of. In so many fields we are beginning to recognise that a holistic approach is the one that brings healing. In the area of health the whole person must be considered. In education the whole child should receive an education for the whole of life, not just facts for passing exams.

For the Christian this sort of health and wholeness is what salvation is about. It has something to do with being truly human.

Ordained to the ministry of word and sacraments, I was inducted to a part-time job under three headings: one was to develop the work of the church and community centre where I am based. The second was to work in the new estates and communities in my town as a development worker. The third heading, which links the other two together, was to be involved in the ongoing worship and sacramental life of the church, in such a way as to put on the agenda of worship the needs of the community and above all to celebrate in the sacraments that Christ is Lord of all and that in him there is 'neither Jew or Greek, slave nor free, male nor female' (Galatians 3:28).

Our church, a Victorian gothic barn, stood in the market-place, an impregnable fortress except for an hour on Sunday morning and the odd concert. Its spire, paid for by a local mill owner on the condition that it should be several feet higher than the parish church spire, pointed to an empty sky. Outside in the town square a statue of Oliver Cromwell pointed gloomily at the recently erected parking metres. Inside was seating for 700 and a dim religious light. Those who sat facing the organ pipes knew each other by which pews they occupied.

Without vision the people perish and this people had vision, and a minister with a flair for creating community centres. (At this point I was training for the ministry, my husband having promised faithfully not to take on any new commitments!)

Several committees, years and grey hairs later, the barn has been gutted, dumper trucks driven through the front door and a floor inserted half way up to create a two-storey building.

The ground floor now comprises an entrance foyer, with a small chapel off it, a spacious hall and kitchen, a small meeting room, toilets big enough for wheelchairs and a room with a medi-bath for the use of the recently established day care centre for the elderly housebound, which is organised by a town committee and part financed by Social Services. A third of the space on one side is occupied by two shops rented out to the public. The rents pay the interest on loans taken out to complete the conversion. A lift or stairs give access to the first floor, which is furnished with a coffee bar, an office and vestry and the hub of the building, the centrum – where worship is held, where the day centre meets, where concerts and plays give pleasure and challenge, where weddings and funerals are celebrated. Our image is no longer the spire, a finger pointing to an empty sky, but a door, ever open like welcoming arms to enfold us, comfort us and push us back out into the world where God is at work.

So the triumphalism of the nineteenth century has been replaced by the concept of the servant church.

The mission of the church has often been based on the model of the ark – a safe refuge in the stormy sea of life – or of a fortress. Down clatters the drawbridge, out rides the Christian soldier into the world to seek and save by bringing back to the safety of the castle all who can be persuaded to come. Then up goes the drawbridge. End of conversation.

Another model has been that of the church – and by that I mean the people not the building – at work in the world, alongside people, enabling reconciliation to happen. When challenged that the church should not be involved in community development, the reply has been that development work (helping people to help themselves) is the work of creating community, redeeming broken relationships, reconciling groups and celebrating life – and if that isn't Christian work, what is?

For us in the church where I am one of the ministers, the model of mission is perhaps that of a warm current in the sea. People are drawn to it. Can Christianity be caught and not taught? Or for many women has this come too late? Has a rigidly structured, male-oriented church driven them away for ever? Or has the privatisation of religion made it a 'feminine' thing, something for 'the wife' to do? To do and to be. To make the tea, arrange the flowers, but never, heaven forbid, preach or serve on the finance committee. Where is the living community of the early church?

If I stand in the foyer of our church centre on a Monday morning I see the middle-aged lady scuttling furtively into the ladies cloakroom. The market trader has sent her in to try on one of his dresses. 'They won't mind, luv,' he says. A harassed mum pushes past me with a pram and a toddler, anxious to deposit both in the shoppers' creche before doing her weekly shop in the market. 'Coffee bar open yet, duck?' asks a large man in an incredible check suit. Jackie, our administrative secretary, rushes past muttering about needing a rota of people to run the rotas. We need over eighty people as volunteers in our building each week. People are beginning to go into the chapel for daily prayers and the day centre clients are cheerfully arriving in wheelchairs and ambulance.

A small boy once threw a stone through a church window and changed the text from 'Glory to God in the Highest' to 'Glory to God in the High Street'. I think the High Street has moved into the church centre this morning. Thank God the church is once more a focus for the cares and concerns of the world. In a minute we will be praying for a local teenage girl and a baby boy both ill with cancer. In our morning liturgy we will reaffirm that:

> The world belongs to the Lord
> *The earth and its people are his*
> How good and how lovely it is
> *To live together in unity.*
> Love and faith come together
> *Justice and peace join hands.*
> If the Lord's disciples keep silence
> *These stones would shout aloud.*
>
> (Iona Community morning liturgy)

After worship, as I share in the morning's chores in the vestry with my husband, who is full time minister here (I'm part-time and only start work at 10 a.m.!), the phone will start to ring.

'Kate, can you visit a woman who brought her child into the clinic yesterday ostensibly to check her weight but really to talk about the death of her father?'

'This is the Doctor's surgery, would one of the ministers visit Mr X? He has now faced up to his terminal illness and wants help in talking to his teenage children.'

'Hallo, can I speak to the Vicar?' 'Speaking, can I help you?' 'I don't want you, dear. Where's your husband?'

'Oh Kate, what can I do? My neighbour's child has just been

run over. It's so unfair. What can I say?'

Is there someone 'up there' enjoying all this? How can a God of love exist alongside the innocent sufferers in this world? Don't tell me suffering is punishment for my sins. That's not my kind of God. Don't tell me it will make me a better person in the long run. It may do, but I don't believe in your vale of sorrows or your refining fire. Don't tell me that from God's eye view it's all part of a plan. If that's his plan I don't want it either.

What can I tell the woman in the cancer ward, the man made redundant yet again, the couple whose child has died? My God is not a puppet master in the sky, leaning from a conveniently placed cloud to manipulate us all. We are free to choose evil and not good and we frequently do.

I start from the premise that wholeness, which means salvation, is our destiny. I see that wholeness on a spectrum that runs through death and beyond into life (I only wish that when pain comes I could feel that always for myself. Help my unbelief, Lord). But I do believe, in the inadequate terms that we use to describe a gracious relationship, that my God is one who endured the suffering of his son upon a cross and that he knows our pain first hand and is with us in our agony.

The Old Testament writers spoke of 'judge' and 'king' but also of 'midwife' and 'nursing mother'. These images of God are all inadequate, but occasionally when you aren't looking, they flash upon the inward eye with comfort and with challenge.

When I talk about day care centres and cancer wards, telephone calls and finances, I am talking about spirituality. I don't see it as something elevated above this life. I see it rather as something deeply rooted in it. Just as I see the signs of God's Kingdom witnessing to love in the community rooted in the world. My husband and I are members of the Iona Community, which grew from a burning desire during the years of depression in the thirties in Scotland to relate worship and the life of the church to the condition of those living in the grim tenements of Clydeside. Fifty years later a community of women and men throughout the world look to the island of Iona with its rebuilt abbey as a source of inspiration and support in their work on the mainland. We are pledged to each other in a financial discipline, a commitment to prayer, Bible study and peace-making. Last summer in Iona some of us took part in an early morning service on 6 August. We celebrated the Feast of the Transfiguration and offered penance that on the same day in 1945 the atomic bomb was dropped on Hiroshima.

The bomb was code-named 'Little Boy' and at the end of our worship we came out of the abbey church to stand in silence round the statue of another little boy – a modern representation of the incarnation. As we stood in the cold grey dawn we heard the bleating of the lambs brought down to the abbey field the night before by the crofters, ready to be taken to the mainland and slaughtered. We heard the lambs and we heard the cooing and fluttering of the white doves in the dovecote above us. The lamb slain . . . the dove, symbol of peace.

Translate that into your community, and mine. During the Falklands crisis three women met on a Tuesday in our town: a Quaker, an atheist and a United Reformed Church elder. They met to share their anguish over the sinking of the *Belgrano* and the *Sheffield*. By Friday forty people had come to a meeting in our church centre and a peace group was formed. If Christians can't be God's peace mongers our witness is lacking a vital dimension of love.

Another sign of the Kingdom – witnessing to God in community.

George has been out of work now for eighteen months. 'Work put boundaries on my day,' he said, 'I'm lost without a timetable. I can make myself useful at home, but it doesn't give me any feeling of achieving anything.' Shades of, 'I'm only a housewife'?

Women who work a full, unpaid day and know how their confidence crumbles, their sense of worth disappears, know how they feel guilty if they seek employment – and guilty if they don't – can identify with the emotional crisis of unemployment. As a sign that a person's worth, their image, is important in God's eyes, our church, like many other churches, is working on several projects. One is a town plan for young unemployed; it may be a palliative but it is important. Another project is group activities and possibly a drop-in centre run by women for women. Play groups and mother and toddler groups are a great deal more than baby-minding or social agencies. They are some of the bricks with which a community is built. All this – peace, worth and what I call joy – are part of the spirituality game. So many people in our society have a deficient sense of identity and belonging. We need to articulate a liturgy of celebration, to create festivals of belonging. The quality of life needs to be enhanced somehow. Joy is a gift. You can't put it on the agenda or plan for it – but it steals in when a stranger is made welcome; it trickles through when an audience enjoys a good night out at a local community theatre group performance. It grows when worship is rooted in the fears, sorrows and triumphs of the community. It abounds when people work together on a common task, when young people and children are accepted as important and equal members of the community. Joy is apparent when opportunities are made for folk to share together round the Lord's table at the Eucharist, at a church weekend, or in cleaning out the gutters. There is spirituality for you.

In my work, celebration is of the essence of what we do. We celebrate life in all its fullness. We're glad that dances and plays, concerts and parties, exhibitions and conferences also take place in the centrum where we worship.

By ordination the church has set me aside to minister in the breaking of the bread and the pouring of the wine. Interpreted in the symbolic meal of those gathered round the table on a Sunday morning or in the ministry of being alongside those who suffer, I am conscious of a strength not my own, but also of my own inadequacy. I am, however, thankfully part of a team, a team not only of those paid to work in the church centre (my colleague ministers and husband, the warden of the day care centre, the supervisor of the play group, the administrative secretary, the cleaners and the caretaker), but also a team of elders ordained to work with the ministers in pastoral care and a team of volunteers trained to work in the groups which use our centre.

Our aim as ministers is not only to shepherd the flock, which means leading from behind as well as in front, not to mention a bit of comforting and prodding, but also to enable this network of care to be established. If the church is a family, the household of God, and not, heaven forbid, a collection of families from which the single or widowed find themselves cast out, then we become a place where 'rent a granny' is possible, where impossible teenagers can seek refuge with other adults away from impossible parents and where the married and single can give and receive friendship which is not threatening.

It is a place of honesty, hugs and hilarity and above it and under it and through it, doing three things at once, as all women know how, is the single parent God providing the mothering and fathering we need.

I came into the church through the influence of the ecumenical movement, the Student Christian Movement and the Iona Community. All three have recently and rightly been concerned with issues raised by an international church consultation held in Sheffield in July 1981.

The issue of sexism had been raised at the World Council of Churches meeting in Nairobi in 1975, but the proposed study of

women's rights and feelings changed in an exciting way to a study
of the community of women and men in church and society.

Women realised that their liberation would not be liberation if
achieved at the expense of anyone else – be it men, poorer women
in the developing countries or children. The study project on the
'Community of Women and Men' became the most widely used
guide ever published by the World Council of Churches. It was
translated into thirteen languages. Discussion throughout the
world culminated in the international consultation, from which a
letter has been sent to churches throughout the world. Phrases
from this letter sum up for me what it is like being a woman priest
in a male-dominated church:

> We learned how deep are the emotions involved in any
> reflection on our being.
> How hard it is to address and envisage God in ways
> that respect the Christian understanding of personhood
> rather than suggest male superiority.
> We rejoiced to recognise that sexuality is not
> opposed to spirituality, but that Christian spirituality is
> one of body, mind and spirit in their wholeness.

The consultation raised the issue of the representation of women
on national and international committees. It pinpointed the hurt
caused by the use of exclusive rather than inclusive language in
worship. It rediscovered the feminine images of God already
present in the Old and New Testaments, but above all it encouraged women to walk tall and rejoice that they are made in the
image of God.

The women and men at Sheffield invite us to pray with them:

> Eternal God, as you created humankind in your image,
> women and men, male and female, renew us in that
> image; God the Holy Spirit by your strength and love

comfort us as those whom a mother comforts.

    Lord Jesus Christ, by your death and resurrection, give us the joy of those for whom pain and suffering become, in hope, the fruitful agony of travail. God the Holy Trinity, grant that together we may enter into new life, your promised rest of achievement and fulfilment – world without end – Amen.

For me it's not being unaware of the depths, the dark night of the soul, but it is an 'activity' not a 'passivity'. For me as an ordained minister in the United Reformed Church it means being active in the peace movement as well as trying to keep the disciplines of prayer and Bible study. It means writing sermons in the car outside the swimming pool or choosing hymns in the dentist's waiting room. It is the hurt and amusement when a small son confides that one minister in the family is quite enough and so he's told his mates that I worked down the pub, or of being introduced yet again as the 'minister's wife'.

Living in faith is perhaps a bit of a juggling act – stirring the soup while preparing a Bible study or greeting worshippers after a service with a child clutching at my cassock skirts.

But walking on the water is, above all, for me an exercise in trust. Trusting not only my husband and sons, friends and community, but also God, to deliver the goods, because without the love, the joy and the peace, as well as the tears and the pain, I'd sink.

P.S. I've told you a bit about the shepherdess. The goats? Still blooming.

Creation

IN THE BEGINNING   IN THE BEGINNING
  THERE WAS DARKNESS
THERE WAS DARKNESS AND THE SEA AND THE
NIGHT
  AND THE SEA AND THE NIGHT
    WERE THE MOTHER.
OUT OF HER MIGHTY WOMB WAS CREATED THE
ALL . . .
    Deep deep inside me, the call for the Mother
      Image ancient, ancient
        far, far away
    God-Mother
      MOON-MOTHER
        Mother of Life – of All
    Rising from the Deep
        the depth
      inside of me – memory of Her – of them
        memory . . .

Monica Sjöö, 1978

Childbirth

Helen Sands

On 7 September 1982, Rosemary Anne Sands was born, at home, in south London. Six weeks later her mother, Helen, recorded a long interview with Sara Maitland: this is a part of that interview. Rosemary and Helen live with Mick, who works for L'Arche, a community for the handicapped, and Amy, who is four.

The trigger for the interview was something Helen had said earlier, that giving birth was like being God, and for her had been a way into understanding more about what God meant. Did she mean the power and sense of creativity?

HELEN: No. I think it is just being *now*; you're just doing totally what you're doing. I think that must be it – the totalness of it. Being the centre of the world – and that's how we could be all the time presumably, but we're not. But this act is just not being distracted anywhere else; and being totally in yourself, being totally present to what is happening. And it is mysterious. I mean this mysterious life which you are going to meet, that is going to come out of you. It's a great work that has to be done, I mean it isn't just on a plate, this great work that has to be done to give birth, to bring to birth, this 'groaning and travail', I mean it is a great act.

And it's funny because it is ordinary too. When we knew that Tuesday evening we were going into labour, there was no panic there, no fear, there were no kinds of special prayers to God or any fancy bits at all, it was just ordinary, we were just doing a job almost – and that in itself was whatever was needed. I didn't pray verbally once – in words or anything. And yet it was obviously a kind of prayer in itself.

Helen did not have a particularly easy pregnancy. She was very sick at the beginning and found a great deal of negativity about being pregnant in herself.

Wanting to become pregnant is wanting and yet not wanting; for me its been like accepting it or going towards it, yet also running away. So that the physical being sick and the awfulness at the beginning doesn't help. It's difficult living with the ambivalence because of the stereotype of motherhood and how marvellous it is. I didn't want to remain stuck with the negativity but it was important to acknowledge it. I remember one evening with Mick going into all the negative aspects of the whole business, not just the pregnancy but what actually comes afterwards, the first three months of constant attention. And I think it quite appalled him what I was saying, because it was so dark and so grim. It wasn't the whole picture but I needed to say that part to get rid of it, exorcise it.

At twelve weeks Helen had a threatened miscarriage.

The strange thing was I had this bleeding in Canterbury Cathedral of all places. It was like a blood clot, so I could feel it coming through. And Mick and I were quite sure we had lost the baby. The strange thing was we were quite accepting of that. Right, this baby has gone, you know. Just like that. So it was as if we hadn't really welcomed this baby, because we were prepared just to let it go. It was hard too – I thought, oh no, we'll have to start all over again. But that seemed strange, the easiness of letting go; perhaps the baby wasn't firmly with us. But there was a real message I think in that. What I had been doing was living the kind of non-pregnant lifestyle and my body just decided not to go along with that, quite rightly. Because I think the beginning is almost more important than the end. I was in bed and I had to rest for quite a long time after that and not be too active, so there was this incredible cut down on activity. I knew I didn't have the strength any more for all the high tension stuff, all the running round on those very tight schedules. Obviously this baby was not going to tolerate it. It was quite sunny some of those days then, I just sat in the sun and Amy would go to nursery school and I'd sit in the sun and Amy would come home and I would have done nothing. But somehow it was okay. It was like the beginning of the holiday.

The rest of the pregnancy was better. When her energy began to return Helen took up yoga in a class designed specially for pregnant women. Both physically and mentally Helen found these classes immensely important.

In the labour I was so attentive. I really knew what my body was up to and where it was tense and I could register that instantly, whereas I could never have done so before.

At thirty-six weeks Helen started 'leaking' amniotic fluid. This, as well as being scary, was especially difficult because home deliveries are not technically 'permitted' before thirty-seven weeks, and staying at home for the birth was very important to Helen.

I'm not sure why it was vitally important; it was a real gut feeling not a thought-out response. I just knew, way before I had Amy even, that I did not want to move into some sterile hospital environment to have a baby. To start something off at home and leave off and go somewhere that I didn't know with people I didn't know, the whole unknownness of it. For me, and for Mick having to go away from something so important; there's no homeliness. I couldn't understand that that would be any good for the labour. The whole thing just seemed . . . crazy.

And it is a shock to go into labour early. I had this vision of nine months – and I mean nine full months. I had this definite picture of what was going to happen. And then I think I had some kind of presentiment. The weekend before it all started I just knew that those three weeks were going to be snatched away from me, and I was really depressed. I said to Mick, look please get all the things out of the loft, and I worked hard right into the night just getting things out and sorting them and I kind of laughed at myself, it really wasn't necessary, but I think I must have known because it was necessary. Because on Monday things started, these leaks of water.

Both the doctor and the midwife were uncertain as to whether these were significant leaks and after a Monday evening consultation it was decided to let things go as they were. By Tuesday evening, however, Helen felt more sure that something was happening.

I felt very taut across my tummy all afternoon – I wasn't sure, but I didn't want to bother people unnecessarily. We had to make decisions, were we going out to dinner? What would happen to Amy? All those decisions that have to be made. And then it was happening and we rang up and said we weren't coming to dinner and then we rang the midwife and she said yes she'd better come. Amy got herself sorted out with a neighbour and decided to sleep there. It all was clear really quite fast.

The stage was set for this event to take place. I lost interest, I abdicated responsibility for anything to do with the outside world. I gave that all to Mick. We were very close, we were very complementary. I was centring and just being inside this body and he was running around getting it organised on the outside.

Then it started and as soon as the midwife came it was up to the bedroom. It was all so fast that I got shivery. I lay on the bed and they got blankets round me and I was quite stricken with coldness. But then I knew that if I got stranded on that bed I'd be there forever. I knew I didn't want to do this delivery lying down. I wanted to be standing up. I said, 'Look, I can't stay here.' They had to help me get off the bed, it was that difficult to move. I think that is a difficulty once you're in labour; in it, it's very difficult to move from one thing to another. Then I was standing up and clasping Mick round the neck facing him, so he was with me the whole time after that. I just needed having my face pressed into his chest, that kind of close contact. I just needed it. And it is the one situation where you can be totally bossy; it doesn't matter because everyone is there to serve you at that moment. I was probably quite nasty, and I didn't feel any qualms about it. If I knew I wanted something I could just say that directly; or if I didn't want something I could be totally 'no' and not polite about it.

One moment I felt very good about: it was in the pushing stage and I knew that the pushing didn't need to be all straining and panting and forcing, that I could just breathe the baby out. I was just in there feeling it and not pushing and just feeling to wait for the next time, and I felt perfectly right. And the assistant midwife said, 'Are you pushing? What are you doing?' And I felt so good that I thought there's no need for me to answer, absolutely no need, I won't answer. And I didn't; I just remained sullenly silent, doing my own thing. Whereas my own midwife didn't ask any questions at all. She was just around what I was doing. And one suggestion she did make – at one point I let out this amazing roar, I really enjoyed that great operatic roar; and I was getting more into the roar than the birth – and she just suggested that I put my chin down and get the energy going down again; if I wanted to roar, kind of roar down. I took that because I knew she knew what she was talking about.

It is an incredible amazing powerful thing. I just remember one point where, between all the – I mean the pain is really pain, bloody hell it is painful – but between some of the contractions and before the pushing I just remember feeling this kind of total exhaustion and absorption; with my face pressed into Mick's chest and there was nothing else I wanted to be doing even though it was like that. There was nothing else I wanted to be doing. I think I felt much more totally giving birth this time because with Amy I remember thinking at one point I don't want to go through this again. And mentally that has a big connection with the body, because I had this very slow transition period with Amy and I think the mental resistance kind of shifts into bodily resistance and slows everything up. Whereas I just wanted to meet this baby really, who had almost bled herself out of me. I really wanted to meet her so there was this great urgency.

And that's a place really where no man can stand, isn't it? And you could say that's sad for the man but it's a unique place to stand. On the other hand, having Mick there, he was a part of that great work very much. I got praise from him and it wasn't kind of 'well done, dear', or 'ten out of ten', it was more a kind of awe of what happened. And holding me . . . maybe that is the male part. The man and woman as an archway and then the woman as an archway for the baby. It all goes on and on forever, doesn't it?

And home, being in our room was another archway. I mean it was totally our room, it was a beautiful room, we had a lovely sunset that evening – we kept the curtains open and we could see that while it was happening and then it was dark when she was born and we'd lit a candle in the room and we had our little kind of altar: we had a very serene Virgin Mary picture, and we had a goddess – your mother goddess.[1] She's doing the birthing primitive earth mother, and the Virgin Mary is post-birth in the way she'd depicted. Also a little cross that Amy made and a kind of plaque I made in clay a long time ago of two hands reaching up to the moon – a moon goddess thing. And just dim light, not much light. It was just like the room was the focus of the whole world then – you know there was no other room in the whole world and people were coming to visit and it was very Bethlehem-like. Amy came straight away and then she wanted to bring her friend Lucy and so Lucy's mum came, so it was like a party straight away. And some of the assistants and the handicapped people from the L'Arche Community came. They arrived very excited, but you know they were completely taken by the atmosphere in the room, completely quiet with it. They were good and alert and made contact with everyone . . . well, it's quite a big thing to come into a birth room, but they were there. It was good and I didn't feel invaded, I felt it was really lovely that they came then. And the doctor came much later from his grand dinner, full of good cheer and alcohol, and he was excited too.

Then they went away and that just left Mick and me and Rosie. Amy was sleeping with the neighbours. So it was very much a house for us. It was nice that Amy slept away, I felt that she gave us that space.

And then we thought about names, we slept a bit, or rested and thought about names, looking up their meanings. We just didn't have one before. People had asked but we didn't have one. She was unknown really. Totally. We thought Rosemary because she had been rosy very fast, very pink; and the dusk had been glowing. And there were nice things to do with Rose – there's a Celtic version of it too, and lots of good connections.

And afterwards, because she was three weeks early, we had to keep her quite warm so the bedroom was the warm room. So I stayed there very much for about five days, just her and me. I ate there and everything, whereas Mick and Amy were in the kitchen. So I was kind of at the top of the house with her and that was really very special. And often it was quite dark. When the darkness came I'd be eating or feeding her, and I was happy to feed and look round and not do anything very much. I wasn't so terribly eager to get back into the world. It was as if we had our special place. I felt magnificent.

Looking Out Towards Sisterhood

Alison Webster

In 1975 Domitila Barrios de Chungara, political organiser, mother of seven and wife of a Bolivian tin miner, went to the International Women's Year conference in Mexico City. At first she was silent, intimidated by the prestige and confidence of the women present, but eventually she spoke out, challenging some of the easy assumptions of oneness among women in a world-wide struggle:

> So I went up to the platform and spoke. I made the women see that they don't live in our world. I made them see that in Bolivia human rights aren't respected . . . that there is what we call the law of the funnel, broad for some, narrow for others . . . that those ladies who got together to play canasta and applaud the government have full guarantees, full support, but women like us, housewives, who get organised to better our people . . . well, we are beaten up and persecuted . . . They [the conference delegates] couldn't see all those things. They couldn't see the suffering of my people. They couldn't see how our *compañeros* are vomiting their lungs out bit by bit in pools of blood. They didn't see how underfed our children are and of course they didn't know, as we do, what it's like to

> get up at four in the morning and go to bed at eleven
> or twelve at night just to be able to get all the
> housework done because of the lousy conditions we
> live in.

This article is an attempt to respond to Domitila's words from both a Christian and a feminist perspective. With the Third World firmly in mind, it starts an analysis of Christian feminism's progress and concerns so far and suggests that there are complicated questions of power and guilt, racism and political commitment that we need to struggle with. Writing it has been hard because I know that women need affirming, not undermining, in the steps we have taken so far. It is easy to shrink from self-criticism. But it is crucial to be more aware than we are of the world-wide dimensions of discrimination.

I start unashamedly from myself and my own story. In the last ten years I have been able to spend several years in countries of the southern hemisphere. The first time was a year's teaching in Cameroun, an ex-French colony a few degrees from the equator. The secondary school that I taught in was caring and stimulating; the nuns spoke of a completely compassionate God and practised this love in their commitment to the pupils. Friends I made there are still friends now. But that year showed me how Christianity has been linked with imperialism and affluence. Church buildings were invariably larger and more solid than any others and church workers better paid. My African pupils, who usually knew the layout of Paris better than the layout of their own home capital, saw that the so-called Christian countries also had the most comfortable lifestyles, and not surprisingly wanted to come to the West. Looking back too I see that sexism was exported by the West along with faith and education. The books I was given to teach from were written for a French *sixième* class and had the usual things – Jane helping her mother ironing in the kitchen while John went out climbing trees and flying model aeroplanes.

Five years later, I went back to Africa and later to India with an ecumenical Christian group from Indonesia, Cameroun, France and the United Kingdom. We spent a year visiting groups of young Tanzanians and Kenyans, listening to their experiences and their urgent questions about the survival and development of their countries. We in our turn tried to share what mattered most to us. Again and again I was confronted by my own wealth and privilege – through having a government which permitted me to travel and a living situation which allowed me to up sticks and go without risking too much. I realised that although we were trying to go without the label of 'teacher' or 'expert' or 'giver of aid', the European members of our group necessarily carried with us the weight of a history which was both benevolent and oppressive. Above all, the journeys crucially changed my sense of what it is to belong in a universal community; I saw with new urgency the need to link the worshipping, contemplative dimension of the Christian life with the demands for social justice that Christ articulates and I saw that the church could be a prophetic as well as a serving community and could anticipate a different kind of world.

Now I am back in the United Kingdom, carving out a niche for myself as a social worker in central London. The new strand for me in the last few years has been an involvement in the women's movement within the church. I have been part of two of the many Christian feminist groups that have sprung up all over the country and that are making a slow but determined attempt to re-evaluate the role of women in the church. Several issues concern us deeply. We are examining the imagery that the Christian community uses in its worship; we are searching for an inclusive language to describe religious experience which will not restrict us to an understanding of God as exclusively male or exclusively female. We are drawing attention to the parts of church structure which are rigidly hierarchical and result in an undervaluing of the ministries of women. We are trying to support those women who have already been ordained and pressing that women in the Anglican Church who have vocations should be considered for the priesthood.

It is often difficult to hold together these different strands of experience and work out an analysis of how racism and sexism operate. What I do know is that I cannot and do not want to slot back casually into a western world view and ignore the ways in which my understanding of faith and the implications for action have been changed by meeting people from the southern hemisphere. I also know that I do not want to have compartments in my life – the Christian, the feminist, the person who has friends in Africa and India. And so, sitting every three weeks or so in our Christian feminist group meetings, I often ask myself what a woman friend from Calcutta or Nairobi would make of our prayer and discussion if she were to turn up. I have a growing sense that so far we have allowed Christian feminism to be limited and diminished by our slowness to understand the perspective of women who do not live in the West.

As white western women, we still have to learn to acknowledge our power. Much of the discussion at present about women in the church emphasises our status as second-class citizens, our long history of being relegated to the church bazaar and the arrangement of the altar flowers. The discussion has both force and accuracy; because the church has been so distrustful and blinkered about the different ministries of women, Christian communities have been seriously impoverished over the centuries. Yet the standard version of the voiceless female member of the congregation loses some of its force when we look at power structures in the countries of the northern and southern hemispheres and at the history of imperialism. As Domitila's words made clear, there is a real way in which we inhabit different worlds.

However we are to define poverty, whether absolutely – in

terms of nutritional levels, or relatively – in terms of access to choice, it is clear that white women in the West have more power. In the United States, it is the wealthy white women who once had authority over the black slaves in the plantations and who rested while their children were looked after by trusty servants. As the Brandt report notes, women are often statistically invisible in development programmes. What evidence there is suggests that they suffer particular hardships compared with the already great hardships suffered by men and boys. In many low income countries, women's life expectancy is lower than men's. More than half suffer from anaemia and in some large poor countries their health appears to be worsening. So-called developments can actually make things worse: some new jobs, for example in clothing or electronics factories, may provide opportunities for women, but when traditional societies are replaced by the modern money system, women's traditional economic contribution is often ignored by the planners, and thus their status is undermined (for instance organising male farmers into trading co-operatives may eliminate the female 'trade' of marketing).

The danger is that being aware of our material wealth and our privilege can easily lead us into guilt – and no further. Each time that I have returned from living in a developing country, I have realised how hard it is to talk constructively in the United Kingdom about the life of the people of, say, Calcutta, without inducing a disabling sense of guilt in the listener or appearing moralistic myself. Those of us who grew up in the 'development decade' of the sixties remember the haunting Oxfam posters – the starving child staring out reproachfully from the advertisement hoarding on the way to school. Over the years, the approach of the aid agencies has become rather different: 'Help the hungry to help themselves . . . Trade not aid . . . It is a question of us, the people of the world, doing something for us, the people of the world' and now the concept of interdependency, illustrated in the Brandt report. But, given a Christian predisposition anyway to feeling bad about things, it can still be very difficult to free ourselves of the liberal guilt which makes us feel responsible for the imperialistic zeal and misdeeds of our forefathers and present governments and makes us feel so helpless today.

Fortunately, our black sisters (so far from mainly outside the church and from the United States) are beginning to say some of these things to us. A book recently published in the States called *This Bridge Called My Back – Writings by Radical Women of Color*[1] raises the question of liberal guilt in the context of a discussion about racism in the women's movement. In one contribution entitled 'An Open Letter to Mary Daly' Audre Lorde writes, 'The history of white women who are unable to hear black women's words or to maintain dialogue with us is long and discouraging,' and comments that at one point in her life she had decided 'never again to speak to white women about racism. I felt it was wasted energy because of their destructive guilt and defensiveness and because whatever I had to say might better be said by white women to one another at far less emotional cost to the speaker and probably with a better hearing.' As Lorde notes, guilt can block communication between us. It can result in the denial of anything outside our own worlds and our own concerns, and allow us to evade any action. We say, 'It's all too difficult to understand, too vast, so let's stick to what we know.'

It seems to me that there are ways, however painful, through this blocking; the Judaeo-Christian concept of reconciliation can offer a path through this impasse, transforming the negativity into growth. In my experience, for example, the ritualising of forgiveness in liturgy can be an important source of healing and openness. I am thinking of a recent service in London when one of our group who had spent many years in the Third World was moving to another city. Seventy or eighty of us met in a rather formal city centre church in London, dimmed the lights and lit candles. We sang, we were still in the presence of God and, towards the end of the time together, we shared a large bowl of rice. The very act of leaving a place in the circle, going into the centre to pick up a handful of cooked rice, was a strong sign of being in union with the peoples for whom rice is a staple and precious food, and perhaps especially with the women who prepare that rice and try to make it go round. I am thinking, too, of a period I spent working in a disused Sikh temple in Calcutta where the dying were brought. All anyone could do was to rub mustard oil into the limbs of the dying, give food and bathe them with water. This place, potentially the most guilt-inducing of all, was filled with the sense of God-given respect for the whole person. Religious labels fell away and ceased to matter as Hindu, Muslim and Christian women and men were cared for to their deaths.

Another way of moving beyond guilt is to enter joyfully into the feminist concept of sisterhood and to look for the commonness of our experiences. One of the things we are learning to do in the women's movement is to tap the riches of myth, to tell our own stories and to discover about women in the Old and New Testaments. The story of Hagar, the slave, follows the story of Ruth, the rich man's wife. The dilemmas are curiously similar to those of our own day: to whom do women owe allegiance – to their country, their men, their children, each other, their own vision? Strongly defined theology is now being written by Asian and Latin American writers who are themselves sensitive to the guilt that Europeans sometimes carry. The Indonesian theologian, Marianne Katoppo, begins her book, *Compassionate and Free – an Asian Woman's Theology*,[2] by commenting that by 1987 the majority of Christians will live in the Third World. 'The countries traditionally seen as Christian will no longer have the numerical advantage. Perhaps then we can finally relieve them of the white man's burden. Perhaps we can finally assert our right to be different and to be the Other.' Writers like Katoppo can help us realise the

positive value of cultures other than our own and with their striking richness of religious language and their ability to draw on
images from everyday life, they can free us from some of our own
solemn and cerebral expressions of faith.

Then there is the need for a political focus within Christian
feminism. The slogan 'The personal is political' was a very necessary cry in the early years of the women's movement when many
women were reluctant to discuss their experience within the home
and when it was evident that women and men could organise
politically in local parties and trade unions without there being real
change in their private relationships and social lives. The slogan
validated a new kind of talk and self-discovery, i.e. what is hard for
me is hard for other women; some of the oppressions women
experience in their daily life stem from societal structures, not from
our own natures. In the growth of women's groups within the
church, these words have had considerable impact. They meant
that the oppressive aspects of the church, the consistent denial of
positive female imagery, was seen to be systemic and to date from
the first century onwards. For many of us, struggling to make
sense of the anger and sense of exclusion we felt in the church,
uncertain whether that anger was legitimate, and often trying as
'peacemakers' to suppress it, it was a revelation to hear other
women speaking.

Christian feminist groups do, of course, vary greatly in how
they have defined their aims and how they have structured the time
together; their strengths do seem to me to lie more in the personal
dimension than in the political. The first group that I belonged to
met about every three weeks, with twelve or so women involved,
and was fundamentally concerned with discussion and reflection.
Two of the women were in theological training, the rest of us
students, or in work. Members of the group took it in turns to
open up discussion, for example, on Rosemary Radford Ruether's
book *New Woman, New Earth*,[3] on imagery in worship, on the

story of Adam and Eve, on the experience of Muslim women in Britain. We also responded to a letter by Una Kroll in the *Guardian* after a decision by the Church of England Synod not to allow women priests lawfully ordained abroad to function as priests in this country. In her letter, Una argued that much of the hostility stemmed from fear and ignorance and suggested that Christian feminist groups all over the country lead times of worship on a Saturday evening. The idea was to give men and women a chance to be part of worship entirely planned and led by women. Numbers were small, but it gave the group a focus for action as well as discussion.

The second group, again with about twelve women involved, is more explicitly personal and centred around prayer. The meetings are times for us to reflect on our daily lives, to share bread and wine and to gain strength from our common faith. We have helped plan special liturgies and have taken part in a festival of women – drama, photographic exhibitions, worship. There is no doubt of the value of such groups. For me, and I expect for most of the women involved, they have been empowering and have provided temporary places to be ourselves, to explore new forms of worship and new lines of discussion. The danger is that we may carry our feelings of safety to an extreme and will be, perhaps rightly, accused of the cosiness into which so many church groups fall. Individual members are involved in other issues, for example, CND, Amnesty International, Child Poverty Action Group. But some Christian feminist groups lack any collective political dimension at all and risk turning into privatised, self-selected encounter groups, which are immensely supportive to their members but also extremely inward-looking.

There is a part of me, too, that still feel uncomfortable at the potentially separatist aspects of Christian feminism. It has been argued that women only groups are necessary in the same way as black consciousness groups in the States in the sixties and in

Britain today are necessary. It is said that we need to meet as blacks, or as women, or as gays, because there is a uniqueness in our experience which even our most sympathetic friends cannot share if they are not victims of these oppressions. I think we do need this time alone to discover ourselves and to gain strength but I think that as Christ came 'that all might be one' the development of separate groups must be seen only as a temporary stage.

Finally, we need to look at the membership and structure of Christian feminist organisation. It is becoming clear that there has been a failure in the women's movement generally, and this includes the Christian feminist movement, to grapple with the perspectives of women who do not live in the West and the disadvantaged black women who do. The majority of women involved in local and national groups are white, middle class and young professional; inevitably they work most urgently and effectively with issues that affect their own lives – the right to abortion, the campaign for equal pay for equal work, the demand for better childcare facilities. But the result of this has been to exclude women whose concerns are different and to give much of the writing coming out of the women's movement a distinctly affluent feel. The obvious example of this divergence in interests has been the campaign for birth control, pursued in the West by women so that they could control their own bodies and their own lives but viewed with profound suspicion by many women in Third World countries. Birth control has been used by imperialist governments and multi-national corporations as a systematic strategy for the social control of the population. As the London-based Latin American women's group writes, 'Politically, the impoverished Latin American masses represent a threat, a revolutionary potential, to the imperialist forces and to the national bourgeoisies.' Edward Galeano's statement: 'It is more hygienic and effective to kill guerilleros in the womb than in the mountains or on the streets' illustrates the crude reality that Third World women have to fear. In the States, where the women's movement grew out of the civil rights movement of the sixties, black women tended to see the women's movement as diversionary. Even international feminist conferences, planned as opportunities for women from all over the world to be heard, have usually been attended by women who are westernised and wealthy – the educated *crème de la crème* of their country. The rich man's club has simply become a rich woman's club.

Some women, of course, like Domitila, have had the courage and the confidence to break into this club and speak of their own lives. My fear is that because Christian feminism has grown out of the western women's movement, we may not hear the voice of Domitila and the thousands like her. We may fall into that institutional racism which puts our own questions first and does not quite get round to looking at the often different priorities of other nations. The feminist who is also a Christian is as likely as anyone to avoid facing her own racism or ignore the covert racism of her own 'radical' group. As we pay careful attention to the sexist nature of much Christian imagery and language used in liturgy, we should note, too, the extent of racist and imperialist imagery. The radical demands of Christ in the Gospel are quite clear, as is the persistency with which he went to the outsiders in his society – women, the poor and the sick. Feminist theologians are beginning to restore women to their rightful place in the Gospel stories – to become, as Elizabeth Moltmann has said, the people who start off church history. One of their finest contributions so far has been the reinterpretation of well-known parables and songs, so that all women can claim them as especially theirs. The Magnificat, for example, is no longer the submissive song sweetly sung by choir boys, but is beginning to be recognised as a strong cry for justice spoken by a pregnant woman who had made a long journey: 'The arrogant of heart and mind, He has put to rout. He has torn imperial powers from their thrones, but the humble have been lifted high. The hungry He has satisfied with good things, the rich sent empty away.' If the Magnificat can become our song too, we will be more likely to remember the special kind of solidarity that being a Christian implies – the knowledge that we are all equal in the eyes of God.

Whatever rhythm of prayer and contemplation we create for ourselves, it must open our eyes and our minds to Domitila and others like her in their search for justice.

Notes

Unless otherwise specified, place of publication is London.

The Dance of the Woman Warrior

1. Maxine Hong Kingston, *The Woman Warrior* (Pan Books, 1981).
2. From a fragment published in *Ecrits Historiques et Politiques* (Paris, Gallimard, 1960) and quoted in ch. 13 of Simone de Petrement's *Simone Weil: A Life* (Oxford, Mowbray, 1977).
3. Monique Wittig, *Les Guerillères* (Women's Press, 1979).
4. Nor Hall, *The Moon and the Virgin* (Women's Press, 1980).
5. Carlos Castaneda, *The Second Ring of Power* (Penguin, 1981).
6. Marina Warner, *Joan of Arc: The Image of Female Heroism* (Weidenfeld and Nicolson, 1981).
7. Sheila MacLeod, *The Art of Starvation* (Virago, 1981).
8. Christine Downing, *The Goddess* (New York, Crossroad Continuum, 1981).
9. *Womanspirit*, number 7/28.
10. Sally Miller Gearhart, *The Wanderground* (Watertown, Mass., Persephone Press, 1979).
11. This story is told on p. 252 of *Meister Eckhart: A Modern Translation* by Raymond Bernard Blakney (New York, Harper and Row, 1941).
12. Carlos Castaneda, *The Eagle's Gift* (Penguin, 1982).
13. Irene Claremont de Castillejo, *Knowing Woman: A Feminine Psychology* (New York, Harper and Row, 1974).

A Sermon Preached at the Women's Mass at Blackfriars, Oxford

1. Mary Daly, *Gyn/Ecology: The Metaethics of Radical Feminism* (Women's Press, 1978).
2. Rosemary Reuther, the Georgia Harkness Professor of Applied Theology at Garrett Evangelical Seminary, Illinois, is an eminent and well-known Roman Catholic feminist liberation theologian.

Growing Up Jewish

1. Natalie Rein, *Daughters of Rachel* (Penguin, 1980).

Poems

1. A year after Alison's illness, the local press carried the story of another child who had been brain damaged in the same way. His parents took legal action and were successful. I contacted their solicitor. He accepted Alison's case straight away. After three and a half years of litigation, in preparation for proceedings in the Crown Court in Newcastle-upon-Tyne, the case was settled out of court. There was no admission of liability. The settlement was for the sum of £100,000. The passage here was written before that settlement was made, and while the whole matter was *sub judice*.

A Faith for Feminists

1. Mary Condren, *Method in Feminist Theology* (unpublished).
2. Mary Daly, *Gyn/Ecology: The Metaethics of Radical Feminism* (Women's Press, 1978).
3. Carol P. Christ and Judith Plaskow (eds.), *Womanspirit Rising: A Feminist Reader in Religion* (New York, Simon & Schuster, 1974).
4. A. Boutet-Mondel, Introduction to Jean-Jacques Rousseau's *Emile* (Everyman edition, 1937).
5. José P. Miranda, *Marx and the Bible: A Critique of the Philosophy of Oppression* (SCM, 1977).

Everything the Pope Ever Wanted to Know about Sex and Didn't Dare to Ask

1. *Gaudium et Spes*, 'A Pastoral Constitution on the Church in the Modern World', Documents of the Second Vatican Council, para 29.

2. 'Sexual Ethics – A Declaration on Certain Questions by the Sacred Congregation for the Doctrine of the Faith' (CTS Pamphlet, 1975).
3. *The New Catechism*, Burns Oates (Herder & Herder, 1967).
4. *New Internationalist*, number 88, June 1980.
5. Rona Reiter (ed.), *Toward an Anthropology of Women* (New York, Monthly Review Press, 1975).
6. 'The Transmission of Life – An Explanation of the Encyclical Humanae Vitae' (CTS Pamphlet, 1969).
7. *Pacem in Terris*, Encyclical Letter of Pope John XXIII, Section 56, (CTS Pamphlet, 1963).
8. *Populorum Progressio*, Encyclical Letter of Pope Paul VI, 1967.

Until the Real Thing Comes Along

1. W.H. Vanstone, *Love's Endeavour, Love's Expense* (Darton, Longman & Todd, 1977).

When Hitler Returns: The Impossibilities of Being a Jewish Woman

1. Mary Douglas, *Purity and Danger* (Routledge & Kegan Paul, 1966).
2. For simplicity's sake I have given the books of the Pentateuch their English names. All references and quotations are taken from the King James version.
3. Mark Zborowski and Elizabeth Greenebaum Herzog, '*Life Is With People*' (New York, 1964), a book about Eastern European Jewish immigrants in the USA.
4. Fifteenth-century code of Jewish law, bringing together and codifying all major Ashkenazi commentary on Jewish law between the first and the fifteenth centuries. Widely adhered to in the present day, it has acquired an almost unchallengeable sanctity.
5. The full dietary ban (Deuteronomy 12:23–25) reads: 'Only be sure that thou eat not the blood: for the blood is the life, and thou may not eat the life with the flesh. Thou shalt not eat it; thou shalt pour it upon the earth as water. Thou shalt not eat it; that it may go well with thee, and with thy children after thee, when thou shalt do that which is right in the sight of the Lord.
6. Leviticus 20:18: 'And if a man shall lie with a woman having her sickness, and shall uncover her nakedness; he hath discovered her fountain, and she hath uncovered the fountain of her blood: and both of them shall be cut off from among their people.'
7. Genesis 19:4–8. The Mishnah asserts that when a man and a woman both stand in danger of defilement, the man must be saved first.
8. Leviticus 12:2–5.

Childbirth

1. For the birth Sara Maitland had lent Helen a Mexican terracotta statue of a birthing goddess: a crude and solid female figure squatting with the baby's head appearing from between her legs. The contrast between this and the traditional 'serene virgin' is very marked.

Looking Out Towards Sisterhood

1. C. Moraga and G. Anzaldua, *This Bridge Called My Back – Writings by Radical Women of Color* (New York, Persephone Press, 1981).
2. M. Katoppo, *Compassionate and Free – An Asian Woman's Theology* (WCC Press, 1981).
3. Rosemary R. Ruether, *New Woman, New Earth* (New York, Seabury Press, 1975).

List of Contributors

Anna Briggs was brought up, the eldest of six girls, in a radical Christian family – as her father's 'only son', directed at a political/parliamentary career (but not at ordination – the radical vision excluded feminism!).

After a time as a city councillor in Leeds, she began to be drawn into a search for the integral relationship between politics, Christianity and living with people. Since being married again to Brian Gallon, who is on the same trail, she has continued working in which ever direction this search has led. She sees issues of health and childbirth, problems of caring for dependant relatives, world development and the nuclear issue as part of the same 'whole' – what is human life *for?* – feels that a feminist approach would transform all forms of human existence, that life is about 'being for others'. She is trying to bring up five children in this spirit. She and Brian are members of the Iona Community and hope to bring the insights of the community's approach to the particular problems of the north-east of England.

Léonie Caldecott is a writer and photographer. Since graduating in 1978, her work has been published in the *Guardian, New Society, Time Out, Over 21*, the *Observer*, the *Sunday Times* and other periodicals. In 1982 she won the Catherine Pakenham Memorial Award for Young Women Journalists.

Her chequered career has also included brief forays into theatre, local radio, TV research and publishing. In the last few years a growing involvement in the eco-feminist and peace movements has taken her as far afield as Japan, and led her to co-edit an anthology, *Reclaim the Earth* (The Women's Press, 1983). She is currently working on *Leave the Apple to Eve*, a book based on encounters with unorthodox Christian and ex-Christian women.

Gail Chester was born in 1951 and has been active in the women's liberation movement since 1970. 'I have mostly lived in London except for three years at Cambridge studying geography and the ruling class, a proud achievement considering my sex, class and religious background. I now work at Ultra Violet Enterprises, a women's collective, promoting radical publications and events. I dream of earning decent wages and of writing influential analyses and inspiring polemics. Pastimes include singing in the Feminist Choir and enlarging my silly jokes repertoire. Confidence to write came from being in the *Women's Report* collective and I have written articles, reviews, conference papers (including 'I call myself a radical feminist' in *No Turning Back* (The Women's Press, 1981) irate letters, leaflets for demos and – with Eileen Cadman and Agnes Pivot – *Rolling Our Own – Women as Printers, Publishers and Distributors* (Minority Press Group, 1981).'

Fiona Cooper was born in 1955. She came to London in 1973 and since then has been active in the women's movement, especially with feminist peace issues. She teaches young women in special education and spends as much time as she can at Greenham Common or working in London for the peace camps.

Meinrad Craighead is a well-known American artist who has lived in England since 1966. Her work has been widely exhibited and she has illustrated books for Collins and The Bodley Head. Two books of her drawings, prose and poetry have been published in England: *The Mother's Birds* (1976) and *The Sign of the Tree* (1979). She is currently preparing a book of images on the theme of God the Mother and she designs engraved doors and windows for churches. She lives in Worcestershire.

Audrey Dunn was born in Hull in 1937. Educated at various primary and secondary schools in Lincolnshire and Hull she went on to office and secretarial work. She later resumed studies at the local College of Further Education going from there to read English at Hull University. This is her first published work. She first encountered God through hard-line evangelicalism. Despite this, and whatever may be said to the contrary, she and God have not abandoned one another.

'Elizabeth' is thirty-three and lives in west London. She currently works in an old peoples' home and on a socialist community newspaper. She felt that there were family pressures against using her real name.

Jo Garcia was born in 1950 and hasn't decided what she wants to be when she grows up. She comes from a clerical family and is now on the fringes of the church. She's a feminist and (still) married; studying maternity and childless so far; a greedy vegetarian with a catholic taste in friends; President-for-life of the Anarcho-Anglican Women's League (membership, one).

Maureen Gilbert was born in Leeds in 1955, the only child of traditionalist Jewish parents who hadn't thought of any girls' names. Compounding her sins by being clever, fat and bespectacled, she survived a miserable childhood and adolescence. Life began at nineteen in the social anthropology department of the London School of Economics. After graduating she held various research and writing jobs in London before moving to youth work in Dublin in 1982. Her main hobbies are cooking and talking. She sees herself as a mixture of hippo and phoenix and her aim in life is to achieve a riotous and colourful form of equilibrium.

Aileen La Tourette was born in Somerville, New Jersey, USA in 1946. 'I had sixteen years of Catholic education, one of which I spent in a convent hostel in Oxford. Came back to England in '68, worked as a journalist, got married in '70, gave birth to Nicholas in '71. Have had three plays broadcast by the BBC, one play performed in Bristol, a smattering of poems published in little mags. Gave birth to Reuben in '75. I now combine waitressing and teaching to support myself, while I continue to be a mother and a writer, not necessarily in that order.

Kate McIlhagga is proud to be a United Reformed Church minister, half a clergy couple, the mother of three sons, community minister at the Free Church Centre in St Ives, Cambridgeshire, a member of the Mastectomy Association and of the Iona Community, a graduate of St Andrew's University, and a woman made in the image of God.

Sara Maitland was born in 1950. She's a writer and journalist and has been involved in the women's movement for twelve years. She'd like to spend her time writing macabre short stories (some of which Journeyman Press are publishing: *Hers, Ancient and Modern*) but as she can't afford to has written a novel, *Daughter of Jerusalem* (1978), a book about women and Christianity, *A Map of the New Country* (1982), and quite a lot of journalism. She's married to a priest and has two children, Mildred (b. 1973) and Adam (b. 1981).

Janet Morley: 'I had a classic liberal education which sharpened my mind but left my female body trundling behind irrelevantly but rebelliously. After graduation and marriage I found myself suddenly agonising between doing research and having babies, activities that seemed irreconcilable. I chose the babies. Pregnancy brought home to me both the low social status and the unacknowledged power of the normal female role. I began to explore feminism, and especially feminist theology. Married to a Methodist minister, but with roots in the Anglican tradition, I am committed to ecumenism and to exploring ways of enabling the laity, and especially women, to exercise responsibility within the church.'

Julia Mosse is making a study of women writers. She has recently spent some time living and working in South India.

Jo Nesbitt was born in Northumberland in 1949, educated at the Convent of the Sacred Heart, and is now recuperating quietly in Holland.

Maggie Redding: 'I was born in July 1939 so am "pre-war" by two months. My mother was a sewing-maid from Hereford, and my father a school caretaker from Southall. Both were Catholic and I was baptised Dolores which I didn't like by the time I was thirty-five and lesbian, so to symbolise another new life I called myself Maggie. I have a daughter and a son who don't understand me and I live with a wonderful person called Sylvia who is also Catholic and lesbian. There are a lot of us about which is why the Catholic Lesbian Sisterhood was formed.'

Michèle Roberts was born in May 1949; she lives alone in London's Notting Hill near the Portobello Road market. She is co-author of the short story anthology *Tales I Tell My Mother* (Journeyman, 1978) and of the poetry anthologies *Cutlasses and Ear-rings* (Playbooks, 1976), *Licking the Bed Clean* (Teeth Imprints, 1978) and *Smile, Smile, Smile, Smile* (Sheba, 1980). Her first novel, *A Piece of the Night*, was published by the Women's Press in 1978. She has just finished a second novel, *The Visitation*, and has begun a third, tentatively entitled *The Wild Girl*. She is currently poetry editor of *City Limits* and teaches here and there.

Helen Sands was born in 1949. She trained as a teacher and has recently been working with elderly women in hospital. She is a committed Roman Catholic, working for change within the church, especially through experimental liturgy and prayer. She is a poet.

Monica Sjöö: 'I was born in the north of Sweden in 1938. I have three sons and have lived off and on in Bristol since 1958. Since the beginnings of the women's movement in 1969 I have worked within it, in the abortion campaign, with unsupported mothers, with lesbian women, etc. Since 1971 I have exhibited and organised with feminist artists and have written innumerable articles about feminist art. Presently four of us have a travelling exhibition called Woman Magic. Celebrating the Goddess within Us' which has been shown around Britain for the past couple of years. The last few years I have concentrated my energies on working with the exhibition and with the matriarchy study groups.

I have, with a New Mexico poet, Barbara Mor, written a book called *The Ancient Religion of the Great Cosmic Mother of All* (Rainbow Press, Trondheim, Norway, 1981). I am now also involved with Fishguard CND.'

Michelene Wandor: Poet, theatre critic, essayist, and playwright for theatre, radio and TV. Her plays include dramatisations of work by Elizabeth Barrett Browning and Radclyffe Hall, and radio features about Antonia White and Dorothy Richardson. She was poetry editor and theatre critic for *Time Out* from 1971–82. Her publications include: (as editor) *The Body Politic, An Anthology of Women's Liberation Writings in Britain 1969–72* (Stage One, 1972); (as editor and co-author) *Cutlasses and Ear-rings, Feminist Poetry* (Playbooks, 1976); (as co-author) *Tales I Tell My Mother, Feminist Short Stories* (Journeyman Press, 1978); (as editor and co-author) *Strike While the Iron Is Hot, Plays about Sexual Politics* (Journeyman Press, 1980); She has also had plays published in *Sink Songs* (Playbooks, 1975) and *Play Nine* (Edward Arnold, 1981) as well as publishing *Upbeat: Poems and Stories* (Journeyman Press, 1982) and *Understudies: A Monograph on Theatre and Sexual Politics* (Eyre Methuen, 1981). She is editor of the series *Plays by Women* (Eyre Methuen, Vol I, 1982, Vol. 2, 1983). Her poetry has been printed in *One Foot on the Mountain* (Onlywomen Press, 1979), *London Lines* (Eyre Methuen, 1982), *Gallery* and *Only Poetry* and other magazines.

Alison Webster was born in 1952. In 1970–71 she taught in Cameroon, West Africa. After taking a degree at Bristol University, she returned to Africa (this time to East Africa) for nine months in 1975. She has also lived and worked in Calcutta. She is now a social worker in central London and is involved in the Christian feminist movement.

Angela West: 'Born in 1945, I attended an Anglican girls' boarding school in Surrey. I taught for a term in Rhodesia in 1964 and returned to Africa in 1970 to teach in a Catholic girls' boarding school in Tanzania.

Meanwhile, I visited China in 1966, graduated from Sussex University in 1967, taught in London and went to Denmark to participate in an experimental education venture with some young Americans I'd met at the Dialectics of Liberation Conference in 1969.

In 1975, I became a Catholic and lived in a community of Catholic radicals in Islington. In 1976 I moved to Oxford where my daughter was born. I now teach English to Asian women, and study theology in the context of the Oxford Christian feminist community. I have contributed several articles to *New Blackfriars* on feminist theology and was a founder member of the Oxford Women's Theology Group.'

Jeanette Winterson was born in Lancashire in 1959. Her formative years were spent as a Pentecostalist preacher and healer until a collapse of commitment caused her to leave the church. After an erratic education and a number of jobs to support herself, she went up to Oxford and read English in 1978. Since graduating she has worked at the Round House theatre, the Gate theatres, for Women in Entertainment and with Cunning Stunts. She operates as a freelance producer, massage therapist and writer. Her most recent project is a book about women as pirates and women as virgins. She lives in London and has no sons.

Margaret Wright has a strong sense of territory and time. She therefore finds herself in conflict with much scientific and technological development which is destroying the first and distorting the second. Supporting women who want home births remains a firm commitment. Joined Ecology Party in 1978, Green CND in 1981.

'Straight' education enables her now to: throw a wet nappy into a bucket from several yards; read very quickly; cease to believe in purely objective understanding.

She has learned most from children. Her greatest satisfactions lie in knowing a poem is ready and repeatable, and keeping a friend at home at the time of birth.

If you would like to know more about Virago books, write to us at 41 William IV Street, London WC2N 4DB for a full catalogue.

Please send a stamped addressed envelope

Book Tokens

**Give them
the pleasure of choosing**
Book Tokens can be bought
and exchanged at most
bookshops.